THE MYSTERY OF THE ONE NEW MAN

DWAIN MILLER

ISBN: 978-0-9846515-8-0

Published by

LIFEBRIDGE
BOOKS
P.O. BOX 49428
CHARLOTTE, NC 28277

Printed in the United States of America.

CONTENTS

FOREWORD BY DR. RON PHILLIPS

— Senior Pastor, Abba's House Church,
Chattanooga, Tennessee

There have been several studies of Paul's '"one new man'" but none compare to Dr. Dwain Miller's enlightening study. Dwain's in depth knowledge of Jewish roots is unrivaled. He blends that with keen insight into endtime prophecy. He is fluent in the Hebrew and Greek so his Biblical insights are right on and true to Holy Scripture.

This book blends classic premillenielism with covenant theology like no other. This wonderful study avoids the extremes of two covenant teaching and the heresy of replacement theology. Dwain's intimate friendship with messianic Jewish leaders add to the fresh revelation offered in this book.

I promise that you will be surprised, challenged, and thrilled with what you will learn from this outstanding scholar-pastor. This teaching has been forged in the fires of a busy pastorate and conference schedule. This teaching grows the people spiritually and the church numerically. Busy pastors will find this material useful and teachable. Lay people will love its clarity and ease of understanding.

Dwain's revelation on baptism has resulted in literally thousands gaining a new hope for a better future. That teaching alone is worth ten times the price of this book.

Dwain comes from a strong Baptist background which guarantees sound doctrine. Like me, Dwain has experienced the mighty baptism in the Holy Spirit and operates in all the gifts. People from across the broad spectrum of the faith will love this book.

Join me in adding this powerful revelation to your library. You will not be disappointed.

FOREWORD BY RABBI CURT LANDRY
House of David Ministries, Grove, Oklahoma

Many people have tried to explore and explain the mystery of Apostle Paul's teaching and often have done a wonderful job of opening our eyes to the deeper things of biblical truth.

However, few have made this attempt with the same personal experience of Dr. Dwain Miller— which uniquely qualifies him for this task.

The teaching within *The Mystery of The One New Man* comes from Dr. Miller's experience of ministering *as* the one new man, not simply ministering *about* the subject of "the one new man."

His life path and knowledge takes the reader into a world of understanding and expectancy and quickly becomes a key to the blessing of unlocking gifts of inheritance found in Messiah.

I have been honored to minister with Dr. Miller for many years now, and I have witnessed that his ability to balance his scholarly understanding and the Holy Spirit is an uncommon gifting that brings forth life-changing revelation.

Dr. Miller has provoked me, a Jewish Believer and pastor, to jealousy with his clarity and anointing that equips him to communicate many aspects of a healthy biblical relationship between the Jewish people and Christians around the world.

Psalm 133:1,3 says: *"Behold how good and pleasant it is for brothers to dwell in unity...for there the Lord commanded a blessing-Life forevermore."*

In this study, Dr. Miller releases you into God's blessing and your inheritance in Him!

Be blessed, friend, and enjoy your new identity as part of the One New Man!

Shalom.

Chapter 1

Opening the Book

*A truly good book attracts very little
favor to itself. It is so true that it teaches
me better than to read it. I must soon lay it
down, and commence living on its hint... What
I began by reading, I must finish by acting. So I
cannot stay to hear a good sermon and applaud
at the conclusion, but shall be half-way to
Thermopylae before that.* [i]

– HENRY DAVID THOREAU

Whitney Cerak was dead. She was buried in her hometown of Gaylord, Michigan, the county seat of Otsego County. A quaint Alpine Village, the city has a total area of 4.0 square miles, and boasts a population of 3,681 people. Her funeral was attended by 1,400 people. Her death had touched nearly half the town.

She and four other of the nine Taylor University students riding with her died when the van they were using to return from a campus event, where they were working as staff, was hit head-on by a semi trailer that had careened across the median of Interstate 69. The accident was bad enough to warrant a section of the Interstate to be completely closed to clear the debris and collect the bodies.

The four survivors experienced head trauma and severe injuries which made them nearly unrecognizable. A coroner was required to identify the body of Cerak and the others. It took four weeks, but, upon receipt of their daughter and sister, the Cerak family held a closed-casket funeral.

At the crash site, a passerby found a girl near the crash struggling to breathe. He helped her as much as he could until the EMT's could arrive. The good Samaritan gave the AirEMT's the purse the girl had been clutching and the helicopter sped off into the night. At the hospital, the doctors, nurses, and staff of the ER attended the young girls injuries.

Meanwhile, other staff began the process of identification. Luckily, they had her purse. Laura Van Ryn's parents were notified and rushed to the hospital. Laura was suffering from level 1 head trauma and brain swelling. She was placed in intensive care where the doctors fought for her life. Barely responsive, Laura was completely unable to communicate with those around her.

As the doctors got young Laura out of immediate danger, the Van Ryn's were given the bad news: their daughter would probably never be the girl they remembered. The head trauma likely caused extensive brain damage, and the structural damage to her bones would render her visage markedly different from the one they remembered.

When her father, Don Van Ryn, entered the room and finally saw his little girl, he saw a body riddled with cuts and bruises, most of her exposed flesh wrapped in bandages, tubes sticking out of her mouth and nose, and wires attached to various parts of her body. The attendant gave the parents her purse and shoes, but informed them that the rest of Laura's clothes had been destroyed as they had to be cut away during emergency triage.

Over the next few weeks, Laura began to slowly recover, members of her family constantly at her side. They even maintained a daily Weblog of her recovery. They enumerated the various small advancements their daughter was making: sipping from a straw to feed herself, indicating a move she wanted to make in playing the game, Connect Four.

Don reported, "While certain things seem to be coming back to her, she still has times where she'll say things that don't make much sense." Then one day, during her physical therapy, the PT asked if Laura could write her name. She raised her still mangled arm and wrote: W-H-I-T-N-E-Y.

Yes, in what is arguably the worst case of mistaken identity in recent history, the two young women had both been misidentified. Whitney Cerak had been undergoing the ministrations of hospital staff and "her family" while Laura Van Ryn lay in a casket beneath a

11

tombstone bearing Whitney's name.

The reasons for this tragic mistake are numerous and understandable. Confusion at the scene, multiple bodies, horrific disfigurement of the bodies and remains, no DNA testing of remains, all of which add up to a tragedy mounted upon a tragedy.[ii]

Sadly, many Christians are living in a similar situation. They have, as believers in Jesus, been given an identity in Christ, but have either forgotten, were never made aware of it, or outright refuse to live in it. They run here and there looking for a way to have a more spiritually fulfilled life, not realizing that the answer has not only been given *to* them, it has already been placed *within* them.

This is what the One New Man is all about, because the "One New Man" is not something you have, it's something that God is doing in you, and, most importantly, it's something you are.

All of this stems from Paul's letter to the church in Ephesus. In chapter 2, he wrote:

> *"But now in Christ Jesus you who formerly were far off have been brought near by the blood of Christ. For He Himself is our peace, who made both groups into one and broke down the barrier of the dividing wall, by abolishing in His flesh the enmity, which is the Law of commandments contained in ordinances, so that in Himself He might make the two into one new man, thus establishing peace, and might*

reconcile them both in one body to God through the cross, by it having put to death the enmity" (Ephesians 2:13-16 NASB).

The Third Day

Some people become offended, confused or even indignant when preachers discuss Greek terms. But there are times when understanding the nuances afforded to us in the original text is vital to our understanding, or, at the very least, our ability to understand original intent. This is true in English as well (as we will see shortly), but in Greek it can mean the difference between having a general understanding of what someone was trying to say and having an understanding that is alive within you.

Take for example a very simple word: *word*. We see it written 637 times in the King James Bible.[iii] But did you know that in the Greek, there are three different words that translate into the English as "word"? They are *logos, grapho* and *rhema*.

The *logos* is probably the most recognizable of these. Jesus is referred to as the logos in the opening of John's gospel. This word refers to something that is said or thought. It is a word that is spoken.

The word *grapho* is actually a little simpler to understand. We get the English word graphite from this same origin. *Grapho*, simply, is any word that is written down or somehow engraved.

It is the final manifestation that concerns us here.

Rhema, on its surface, simply refers to an utterance. But it is so much more than that. Rhema happens when the *grapho*, turns into *logos* and, through a quickening by the Holy Spirit makes a word come alive in a person!

The "One New Man" is not some new spiritual wave or religious movement, doctrine, or theology. It's been in the Bible, we just haven't seen it. It has only recently become *rhema* in the Church. Now is the day for this message to be revealed, because we are living in the third day. In the book of Hosea, the prophet decreed:

> *"Come, let us return to the LORD. For He has torn us, but He will heal us; He has wounded us, but He will bandage us. He will revive us after two days; He will raise us up on the third day, that we may live before Him"* (Hosea 6:1-2 NASB).

This is a declaration that, prophetically, there would be a time of two "days" wherein God's people would live in an age of grace, but then a third "day" would arrive and God's people would be "raised up."

A day with God is as a thousand years and a thousand years a day, and it has been approximately 2,000 years since Christ's arrival in physical form and departure in glorified form from this earth. I believe we are living in the third day of Hosea's prophecy.

In the third day, the revelation of the One New

Man will finally become a reality. All this means is that, in the third day, we will understand who we are in Christ, everything His blood covenant has given us, we will start exercising through faith who we are, and finally stop walking around as wimpy, whining, defeated Christians. Instead, we will be a bride so filled with His glory and so in love with Jesus that when He comes back He will recognize us, and, in us, the world will see that Jesus is a conquering Savior!

I sometimes think that, if Jesus looked down at most Christians in America today, He might ask Himself, "I wonder what I died for? These people look all beaten up." The Lord is returning for the Church Triumphant not the Church Trampled!

And the worst part of this is that Christians walk around with a feeling they are in constant combat; but the enemy they fear to face has already been vanquished. The greatest news is that everything you need, Jesus has already accomplished. You don't have to talk the Son of God into doing anything for you, because He's already done it. So, if there's a discrepancy between what He's done and where we are, the discrepancy is ours not His.

Before reading another word, ask yourself this question: Would I like to have everything that Jesus died to give me? If the answer is yes, continue on!

Is this about discipleship? Yes. But it's much simpler than what that word conveys. This is really about overcoming victorious Christian living which is the result of the One New Man. You receive the One New

Man by birth. When you are born again, it's yours. It is who you are. The receiving of it is based upon what you do with that revelation.

In America today, we have a brutal misunderstanding of God's Word. For example, take the following verse:

> *"Jesus told the people who had faith in him, 'If you keep on obeying what I have said, you truly are my disciples. You will know the truth, and the truth will set you free'"* (John 8:31-32 CEV).

Now think about how many times you've heard the final phrase of Jesus' statement: "The truth will set you free."

I performed a cursory web search for that phrase and found some interesting quotes. For example:

- President James A. Garfield said, "The truth will set you free, but first it will make you miserable."
- Famous lawyer and leading member of the American Civil Liberties Union, Clarence Darrow, said, "The pursuit of truth will set you free; even if you never catch up with it."
- Entertainment mogul Oprah Winfrey said, "The thing you fear most has no power. Your fear of it is what has the power. Facing the truth really will set you free." [iv]

Most of these comments sound intelligent and noteworthy, and, yet, every one of these statements is completely wrong. You see, Jesus didn't just say that "the truth [would] set you free." His words were conditional.

First, for the statement to be true there was a condition of membership. You had to be a disciple of Jesus. In order to be a disciple you had to engage in a condition of action. Specifically, you had to continue on in obedience to all that Jesus had said. Finally, if these conditions were met, then and only then would you know the truth. And it was the knowing that would perform a great miracle in your life. You see, it isn't simply *truth* that sets you free; it's *knowing and accepting the Truth.*

Who Are You?

All of this is about our identity in Christ. In his letter to the Galatians, Paul wrote:

> *"I have been crucified with Christ; it is no longer I who live, but Christ lives in me; and the life which I now live in the flesh I live by faith in the Son of God, who loved me and gave Himself for me"* (Galatians 2:20 NASB).

This verse is the statement of our condition in the reality of the One New Man. And it sounds great! But sounding good doesn't help you know how to live it.

To get the *rhema*, start by breaking down the verse into its individual statements.

I Have Been Crucified With Christ

Read that again! When were you crucified? "I *have been...*" This use of the verb is in what's called the present perfect tense. What this means is that the verb designates an action or occurrence which has already happened, but which continues into the present or the effect of which is still ongoing. This means that, in Christ, I am crucified with Him. The question is, am I living like I am a crucified man?

It Is No Longer I Who Live

This is difficult, and we will discuss it more at length later, but, put plainly, this means that, in Christ you are dead.

But Christ Lives In Me

What this signifies is that, even though I am dead, I am alive because Christ has chosen to live in me. I am empowered and made alive by the same One who spoke all of creation into existence.

The Life Which I Now Live In The Flesh

I live NOW! I can't live in yesterday! Some of us

dwell in the past and *that's the problem*! You can't control or change tomorrow, whether the sun will come up or not, whether there will be rain. Jesus wants to come and help you NOW! We must live in the NOW!

I never get upset when people get "in the flesh"; that's all they have. We don't possess a glorified body; we have a body of flesh. Sometimes, it rears its ugly head, but that doesn't mean the flesh has to control you.

Sadly, most Christians are living under control of the flesh. We have churches and whole religious movements in America that have watered down the blood covenant, pilfered the gospel just to try to make people feel good, not just in general, but about living in the flesh.

I don't know about you, but I war with my flesh, because it is the thing that the devil wants to use to steal, kill, and destroy my reward and covenant. He's not so concerned with taking me to Hell as he is with making me live in Hell now! It is a frustrating truth that some of you haven't gotten past the fact that Jesus didn't just die to keep you out of Hell, He died to give you everything that Adam cost you.

When Adam lay there in the cool of the Garden of Eden, God had bestowed upon him the power to tend the plants of the garden in a way that was near effortless; he was granted dominion over the living things even to the point of being allowed to name them; he was granted the liberty to commune personally with God. It was, in many ways, Heaven on earth.

When the second Adam, Jesus, came, part of His mission was to restore what Adam lost. God wants you to have some of Heaven RIGHT NOW! Do you want to enjoy and delight in some of Heaven today? It's your choice. You have to choose to live in it!

From Condition To Position

So that's who you are in Christ. How then do you move from where you are into the truth, power, and glory of what you are in Him? You see, as far as God is concerned, you are already seated with Him in Heavenly places (Ephesians 2:6). Why do you wander around on this earth acting, feeling, and believing that you're living in Hell when all the time you are actually sitting on Daddy's lap in Heaven?

This is about what the Bible says, not what your theology teaches, not what your church preaches, not what your granddaddy taught you. It is my hope that, as you read the words of this book, as they align with Scripture, the Holy Spirit will anoint you in a fresh way to break every religious spirit that has come and lied to you in order to steal from you. The devil doesn't care how many days you live as long as you don't live the days you have. When you wake up and understand who you are in Christ, the devil doesn't stand a chance!

This is what the third day revival is all about. It's a

time for us to understand who we are, what we have, and we stop treating God like a spiritual ATM trying to get Him to give us what He has already deposited within us.

We must repent and understand that Jesus didn't come to condemn, and repentance isn't a negative word. It means, simply, to return to a correct way of thinking. When we repent of our error, whatever that may be, God is sure to forgive us and, more than that, He sets our feet back on the correct path so that, as we draw near to Him, He will draw near to us.

CHAPTER 2

NAILED TO A CROSS

*The nature of Christ's salvation is
woefully misrepresented by the present-day
evangelist. He announces a Savior from Hell rather
than a Savior from sin. And that is why so many
are fatally deceived, for there are multitudes
who wish to escape the Lake of fire who
have no desire to be delivered from
their carnality and worldliness.* [v]

— ARTHUR W. PINK

Bill Gaither had quite a hit with the song "I'm Just a Sinner saved by Grace," but, as much as I love Bill Gaither, his music and the work he's done for the Kingdom, he was mistaken. It's a little thing, but the "I'm" or "I am" in that title is what makes it egregiously wrong.

When you say "I am" you are making a statement of present condition. "I am a big football fan." "I am a fast driver." "I am currently on a strict exercise regimen." These "I am" statements convey *current status*. In Gaither's song, what that title implied and what is sung in every chorus is this statement: "I am currently an active sinner, but God's grace saved me." This is simply not correct. It is true that I *was* a sinner, but I was saved out of that misguided and fallen state by God's amazing grace! According to the Bible, I am—currently, right now this moment—the righteousness of God (2 Corinthians 5:21), a saint (Ephesians 5:3), a member of a royal priesthood (1 Peter 2:9), and a joint heir with Jesus (Romans 8:17).

Let this next statement be *rhema* for you! If you want to live according to the economy, the mindset, and the theology of this world, to be broke, busted, and disgusted, that's your prerogative!

It's already been pointed out that, in Christ, we are dead because we have been crucified with Him. In his letter to the church at Rome, Paul quoted the psalmist and said, *"As it is written, 'For your sake we are being killed all the day long; we are regarded as sheep to be slaughtered.'"* (Romans 8:36 NASB).

That is the truth of the Christian life. But if you choose to trust God, you will no longer be a sinner, but a saint; no longer selfish, but selfless; no longer sick, but whole; no longer bound, but set free; no longer defeated, but victorious, in Jesus name! But you MUST begin with a crucified life. Part of this is remembering to *"present your [body] as [a] living sacrifice"* (Romans 12:1).

A father of mine in the faith once told me that the problem with living sacrifices is that they too often try to wiggle off of the altar. To live the crucified life, you have to lay yourself willfully on the altar and count yourself as one slaughtered for God.

It isn't easy. In fact, it is often painful. It takes discipline, and we as a human race find it sorely lacking. It is our lack of self-control that not only prevents us from embracing the One New Man, but hinders us from understanding much of God's truth as He has so graciously set forth in His Word.

Remember that Galatians 2:20 says that I have been crucified. It's past tense! It has already happened. I am dead. If you're born again, then you're dead! Out of my Baptist heritage, I never had to struggle with this concept. I was taught that I was dead my whole life. So, if you've been crucified and are "dead," how does that affect your everyday life?

You Have Died To Sin

The book of Romans is the Apostle Paul's grand masterpiece of Christian Theology. It is so complete yet clear in its explanation of the Christian life that we have seen the great evangelistic tool "The Romans Road" come out of its pages.

In chapter 6 of that book, Paul asks a series of questions that directly impact our understanding of the crucified life. In verses 1-2, Paul asks, "what shall we say then? Shall we continue in sin that grace may abound? Certainly not! How shall we who *died to sin* live any longer in it?" [emphasis mine]

Please understand. If you are in Christ, then when Jesus was placed on the cross, you were on the cross with Him; when He died, you died. Romans 6 asks the question, shall we continue in sin so that grace may abound? The idea is that some were teaching that to sin was a good thing because if you did you were then able to take a fresh measure of God's grace.

The book of Romans answers this and says "God Forbid!" It's wrong! Not because it will send you to Hell, but because it will make you live in Hell right now! There are consequences to not living in the reality of who you are in Christ.

Again, when Jesus died, YOU DIED! When you repented, at that moment, as far as God was concerned, from the foundation of the world, you got on the cross, you were nailed to the tree, and the body of sin that was sending you to Hell was borne completely in Jesus' flesh and His blood, and He bore your death. You died! So how can you, who are dead, sin and keep living in sin?

There is theology currently alive and growing in the Church that says we have two natures, the old and the new, the flesh and the spirit. If you are born again, you don't have two natures. The old nature was nailed to the cross. Knowing this, your old man—who you used to be—was crucified. He is dead.

How? In the mind of God, before the creation of this world, it happened. With this, we tend to get into the theology of predestination, which is, of course, an understandably difficult topic. But this truth didn't do away with free will.

God predetermined that every person would be born again. He has a book of life, and in it is written the name of every individual who has ever lived or ever will live. In Revelation we are told "their name was blotted out of the book." This means it was already there.

Your Heavenly Father gave you free will so that you can decide, but it is HIS free will that we come to Him. And He predetermined that every one of us CAN have eternal life with Him. But if you choose to reject Him, Jesus, and the sacrificial atonement provided for you at Calvary, *then* your name is blotted out of the book.

Be clear, God has never chosen some for Heaven and others for Hell. Jesus died for the sin of the entire world!

A Unified Vision

Your salvation is lived out in two ways: (1) in God's perspective and (2) in your perspective. When your vision matches God's vision, then you will live and walk in complete victory.

You see, when Jesus died, the curse that sin brought to the earth and the inherent sin nature was dealt with by His blood. And the reason the enemy hates the message of the cross, repentance, and the blood is because that's the only way you can enter into the crucified, overcoming life.

You can't achieve this through religion. You can't do it through self. You can't pray enough prayers. You can't get baptized enough to wash it all away. You can't join enough churches. You have to climb up on the cross of Calvary and DIE!

When you do, you are free! (Romans 6:7). For sin shall not have dominion over you (verse 14).

So often I hear people say words such as, "I am an addict and that's just how it is because I have a sickness that was passed on to me from my parents," or "I'm a homosexual. It's who I am, and I was born this way." or "I guess, technically, I cheat on my spouse, but that's just the way it is. I don't have it in me to be monogamous."

I am telling you now that every one of these statements is a lie from Hell! In Christ you can be set free from all of these sins, and more, because the blood of Jesus kills and buries that curse. But it can only happen if we die as well.

When we die, so does the temptation of sin, we cannot be antagonized. That's because sin, sickness, fear, torment, addiction, and all of these evils have no ability to affect a dead person.

You Have Died To Sickness

In test screenings for his film, *The Passion Of The Christ*, Mel Gibson distributed questionnaires to specially invited viewers. One of them was a pastor. In response to the question, "Do you see any misalignment with Scripture in the film?" the pastor responded, "Only one. When he was on the cross I could still recognize the actor, Jim Caviezel, but the Bible indicates that Jesus was so marred by the beatings He endured that there wasn't a strip of skin still whole on His body and, in fact, His visage was so destroyed that He was absolutely unrecognizable."

I often think about the Roman cat o' nine tails. It really was one of the most horrific devices of punishment ever made. Leather strips stretched out from a long braided handle. Each strand inlaid with bits of pottery and sharp stone, a small but heavy metal ball was tied into the end of each strand, and stretched out from that was a small hook. The effect was brutal. As the ball struck the skin it caused excessive bruising. The hook then dug into that area and pierced the flesh and sliced it open, while the fragments of pottery and stone insured that the skin was ripe for more tearing and bleeding. [vi]

The Bible says that it was these stripes that provided our healing. How is that possible? I don't claim to have all the answers, but the Bible again and again refers to the stripes. In the Apostle Peter's first letter, he wrote:

> *[Jesus] bore our sins in His own body on the tree, that we having died to sins, might live for righteousness—by whose stripes you were healed"* (I Peter 2:4 NASB).

29

Again, notice the small important words. When did you get healed? It is in the past progressive tense. This tense indicates that at the very moment Jesus was being whipped, you were being healed.

Yes, I believe in healing. I hear people accuse us at Cross Life Church—and, incidentally, accusing other Christians who share our belief in healing—all the time of arrogance, that we think we can just lay our hands on anybody and they'll be healed. People never get healed just because I lay my hands on them. I cannot heal any person, but I do believe that their healing has already been delivered to them!

Jesus has already paid the price. So I have faith that you will be healed when I pray for you, but it's not my authority to heal you. It's only my business to believe what the Word says. I have been asked, "What if you pray for them and they die anyway?" Well, they received their Heavenly healing, didn't they? And, it was the best healing possible!

Perhaps you have been hurt and abused; you've been rejected. But when we're crucified, all of our STUFF—our emotional wounds—gets healed.

One of the things that's cursing America today is the spirit of orphanhood. We don't understand who we are, we don't understand authority, and we don't comprehend this because of our own actions; we have been abandoned spiritually.

This abandonment has created a chaos of self-centeredness in our nation. And the church has responded by making the Christian life a spiritual buffet, dishing out a little bit of everything making sure its attendees get exactly what they want or they won't come back for seconds. This is crippling the church, and harming the people it is supposed to be raising up, nurturing and preparing to be overcomers.

You Have Died To Self

Remember that phrase in Galatians 2:20? It is no longer I who live, but Christ lives in me. I have said several times in the few pages so far that the single most important thing you must understand to live the life that Christ intends for you is that you are dead. But you aren't really dead, are you?

This is one of those paradoxes of our faith. Just like if we wish to be free, we must be a slave to Christ; we are royalty, and yet we are mere clay in the Potter's hands; we are alive in Christ only when we die. Yes, I am physically alive, but, according to God's Word, it's not me doing the living. It is, instead, Christ *in* me! If you're born again, Christ is in you!

The best part of this is that Jesus didn't come into your life in installments. He didn't just enter as Savior to keep you out of Hell; He came in as Lord to be a Righteous Ruler of your life; He came in as Priest to minister to your needs; He came in as Righteous Judge who declared you innocent in His sight; He came in and brought all of His Kingdom, power, dominion, and glory.

The question is not and has never been, "Is He in

31

you?" The real question is, "Are you in Him?"

The sad lie religion tells us is that Jesus came to keep us from Hell. Yes, He died so you wouldn't have to spend eternity in Hell, but that's not why He came. Jesus died on the cross and was resurrected to reverse in you everything that sin and the curse cost you, to make you a trophy of His grace and a testimony of His power.

When Jesus hung on the cross, He felt the piercing of the nails in His hands and feet, He felt the pain of the thorns on his brow, and the untold agony as He was whip-lashed and beaten. He felt the sting as the hairs of His beard were ripped out of his face. He felt the intense torment every time a piece of dirt entered one of the many open wounds on His body. He endured the indignity of the soldiers spit running down His face.

But there came a moment when all of that pain ceased. It was when He died. When they rammed the spear into His side and the blood and water gushed out, Jesus did not feel that because He wasn't even there—He was with His Father in Heaven.

Do you know how to go through life not being offended, hurt, rejected, abandoned, addicted, and bound? Die! It's impossible for the devil to tempt a dead man.

CHAPTER 3

FOREVER CHANGED

*If you would attain to what you are
not yet, you must always be displeased
by what you are. For where you are pleased
with yourself there you have remained. Keep
adding, keep walking, keep advancing; do
not stop, do not turn back, do not turn
from the straight road.* [vii]

— SAINT AUGUSTINE

T he chill was already in the air that late November day in Chicago, as Sarah Dunn Clarke boarded the train bound for Omaha. But Mrs. Clarke was not a passenger; she was on a mission. Sarah spotted her quarry seated next to a swarthy man dressed in crisp clothing.

The young woman Sarah was searching for was the daughter of a wealthy, prominent London banker, and the man she was with had kidnaped her with the intention of adding her to his "disreputable house" in Omaha.

Mrs. Clarke and her companion, Mr. Blackburn,

confronted the pair, and, without many words spoken, Sarah grabbed the young woman and escorted her off the train just as it started its journey west.

It all began in the early 1860s as Sarah Dunn was working to prepare an elaborate redecoration of her family's home in Waterloo, Iowa. While in the process, she is said to have heard an audible voice ask, "What are you doing to decorate your Heavenly home?"

It was the thought of the endless streak of perishing souls trudging toward Hell, doomed to spend an eternity without Christ that drove Sarah to Chicago to found the Pacific Garden Mission in the midst of one of the most notorious areas of Chicago. Every night some 5,000 men would find cheap lodgings in the flophouses of Murderer's Row, while all around the wares of drink and sex were peddled, sometimes right in front of the PGM.

Today, some 150 years later, the Pacific Garden Mission is still active in the community of Chicago, where it provides refuge and relief to hundreds every month. The history of lives changed due to the ministry of Pacific Garden Mission is heard on over 1,100 radio stations on the broadcast drama "Unshackled." And it's all due to the change brought about in the life of Sarah Dunn, when she responded to the call of her Savior. [viii]

This is the effect of a crucified life. It becomes a life not only changed but *exchanged.*

In and Of

"And the life I now live in the flesh..." we have already covered at length, but the next phrase is even more important primarily because of the promise that it conveys and the problem found in the translation of it. Paul says that the life he lives he "live[s] by faith in the son of God, who loved me and gave Himself for me."

This is a wonderful thing, and it is certainly true, but this is another instance where little words mean a lot, and not every translation of the Bible gets it right. This phrase is better translated this way: "And the life which I now live in the flesh, I live by *the* faith *of* the Son of God."

Do you see the difference? It's one thing for us to have faith in Jesus. We should have that, and yes it is a gift from God in and of itself. But what Paul says here is that the thing that enables him, enables us, to live the crucified life, changed life, is not *our* faith but the faith of Jesus Christ Himself!

The fact is you don't even have to have enough faith to live this life in yourself. You can't live this life by your own power. But Jesus gives you the faith to live in Him, and that is what gives the overcoming power that you need to be who He has made you to be.

The faith comes from Him! You didn't even have enough faith, in yourself, to get saved. God gave you that faith! "For it is by grace that you are saved through faith!" (Ephesians 2:8).

The faith of the Son of God in you empowers you to live the life He wants you to live, and that faith helps you to believe what He says about you. Of course, you already know what your flesh says about you; but you're not in your flesh, you are in Him. You know about your past; but you're not in your past, you are in the "right now" in Him. You don't even have to give an ear to what your father, your mother, husband, wife, friends, enemies, exes, or the world says about you. You must, in Christ, turn your attention to what the Bible says about you.

Believe—through the faith of Jesus, not your own faith—that what the Bible says about you is true, that you are who you are by the grace of God!

The Bible says you are no longer what you used to be, and you presently aren't what you're going to become, but by His faith you are everything He wants you to be. It's by His faith, the faith of the Son of God, that you live.

The Exchanged Life

There is an endless stream of talk on television, radio, and print media about the importance of diet, and it's nothing to hear conflicting stories back to back. There are meat diets, juice diets, vegan diets, popcorn and orange juice only diets, dietary supplements, organic, probiotic, herbs, micronutrients, macro-nutrients... It's SO confusing!

What we do know, however, is that "you eat or you die." But the sad truth is that if you fed your body the way you feed your soul with the Word of God, you'd either be on life support or already dead!

The Ex-changed life is a daily process. You have to believe what the Word says, but to know what's on its pages, you have to hear or read what is written in the Word.

In the second letter to the Corinthians, Paul wrote these amazing words:

> *"Therefore from now on we recognize no one according to the flesh; even though we have known Christ according to the flesh, yet now we know Him in this way no longer. Therefore if anyone is in Christ, he is a new creature; the old things passed away; behold, new things have come"* (2 Corinthians 5:16-17 NASB).

The new has arrived! The old is gone! If you want to search the planet and take twelve steps to get healed from your addiction, that's your choice, but if you will just find your place in Christ, He can do away with the problem through His faith in a moment and you can be delivered instantly!

In the Greek, this word "new" is the word *kainos*. This is an insightful word in Greek, and, much like the word "word," this is not the only term we translate as "new." So what does it mean?

Imagine that it is an early spring day. Winter has come and gone, the grass, and weeds, have taken in the warming sun and rain and have grown. You decide that today is the perfect time to get out there and mow the lawn. You oil up the lawnmower and fill it with gas, spilling some on you in the process. You cut the grass and edge the driveway and sidewalks. You get out the blower and rake to clean up the clippings. You kneel down on your knees in the dirt of your flowerbeds and pull the weeds.

At the end of the day, your lawn looks beautiful while you look horrible! You are covered with grime, and the salty perspiration of your hard work. There are cuts and scrapes on your arms and legs from flying pebbles caught by the wire of the weed eater. There is only one thing to do: it's time for a shower.

You make your way to bathroom, remove the soiled clothes and step into the steaming shower. You use your favorite body wash and shampoo and let the hot water and soap wash all of that grim down the drain. The water rinses the suds away and you step out of the shower thinking, "I feel like a new man!"

That is *kainos*. You have been changed from the filthy thing you were into a refreshed version of yourself. When Jesus comes and makes all things new, you are still you, but all of the old junk is gone and He has made you brand new!

How is that possible? Paul answers this question later in 2 Corinthians 5 when he says:

"[God] made Him [Jesus] who knew NO SIN to be sin on our behalf, so that we might become the righteousness of God in Him" (2 Corinthians 5:21 NASB).

Because God made Jesus, Who knew no sin, to be your sin for you, every evil thing you have ever done or even thought about doing, Jesus became *that* on the cross. So, even though Jesus never sinned, He took your sin and had it placed on Him by God.

As a result, Christ made it possible for God to transfer that righteousness to your spirit. What that means is, in Christ, you are, right now, as Holy as you will ever be. Because when God looks at you He sees the perfect righteousness of the One who knew no sin.

You worry, "You just don't know what I really did when nobody was looking." That's your flesh speaking —and you need it to be disciplined. The great thing is that because of who you are in Christ, you have both the power and authority to do that. However, if you can't, you may not be born again, and that is something you need to deal with immediately!

Just as you have to bathe and change clothes every day or there are some negative side effects, you have to take off the old man of the day and put on a new one. Spiritually, it's the same way. You have to remove the old man daily and put on Christ. You need to be made *kainos* (new), refreshed, every day. How is this possible? It's part of repentance or the changing of your mind.

39

Paul wrote in Romans 12:

"And do not be conformed to this world, but be transformed by the renewing of your mind, so that you may prove what the will of God is, that which is good and acceptable and perfect" (Romans 12:2 NASB).

The problem is that, too often, we allow ourselves to say, "This is who I am" or "This is what I want." Well, that's the real problem. When we are conformed to the world, we can't allow God to change us. Do you have negative thoughts and feelings? If the answer is *yes*, you need to kill those feelings. You'll have a better relationship with your spouse if you will die to self. You'll have a better work ethic, be a better husband, wife, father, mother, employee, neighbor, citizen, if you will just die as Scripture declares!

When you are prepared to do this, you will live the crucified life; God's Son will step in and change you. And the faith of Jesus is the exchange. As far as the Lord is concerned: You are no longer in the flesh! You are a new creation! He became your sin, so you have His righteousness!

When you embrace the crucified life, allow God to change you and bring you into the revelation of the One New Man, you do so because you live in the flesh by the faith *of* the Son of God!

CHAPTER 4

GET YOURSELF
CONNECTED

*Just as the wave cannot exist for itself,
but is ever a part of the heaving surface
of the ocean, so must I never live my life
for itself, but always in the experience
which is going on around me.* [ix]
— ALBERT SCHWEITZER

Santa Cruz de la Sierra, Bolivia, is the capital of the
Santa Cruz department in eastern Bolivia and the
largest city in the country. Boasting a total population
of 2.1 million citizens in the metro area, Santa Cruz
nevertheless is only 207 square miles.

Somewhere, lost in the sprawl of the city, sleeps
Tomas Martinez. Tomas has made some poor choices
in his life. He has experienced the malaise of alcohol
and drug addictions. The effects of these conditions
have led him to be a vagrant living on the streets of the
city.

It is always difficult to track down a homeless
person, but Tomas Martinez has made it even harder

41

for the authorities. He is actively eluding them out of fear he is being hunted down in an effort to prosecute him for activities committed as a result of his alcohol and drug-related habits. The last anyone saw of Tomas, he was running away from the police.

The problem is that the police were not, in fact, chasing down Tomas to arrest him, but to alert him that his estranged wife, Ines Gajardo Olivares had died and left him a sum of $6 million dollars. Yes, Tomas Martinez, the homeless millionaire, is currently walking the streets of Santa Cruz de la Sierra with no place to lay his head, scrounging for food and drink, fighting off the cold nights with found clothing "paradoxically not knowing his fortune."[x]

How like this man we are. We who believe in God, have accepted Christ's sacrifice and atoning work at Calvary, have received the promise of the Holy Spirit, claim to believe in the provision of our Heavenly Father, and yet walk around completely disconnected from our own fortune?

Like Tomas Martinez, many Christians live their lives separated from their own provision. How often do we hear from people who say things such as, "I go to church all the time," "I'm always at my church…," "My church says…," "At my church we teach…," or the worst one I've ever heard, "I finally connected with a church."

Please don't misunderstand me, none of these things are bad, necessarily, but the prominence of these statements demonstrate a fundamental flaw in the thinking of a Christian.

The church is not first and foremost what you were connected to. You were connected to God's Kingdom *in its totality*. And the problem we have in understanding this in America, is that we are a democracy. We love our democracy. We cherish the fact that every person has a voice. But God's Kingdom is a theocracy, and how it works is that the King owns everything. When you yielded to Him, He provided it all.

God must have a hard time recognizing most Christians in His Kingdom because they are living with such a mentality of poverty, misery, and defeat. However, when you realize that you are brought into His Kingdom then you begin to understand that everything He has is yours!

Far too many believers get hung up over tithing. Let me just say that one of the things I love about tithing is that it is a clear indication of how much you trust God. Jesus said you can serve God or money, but not both, and every time you take out your wallet, your checkbook, or your debit card, and give your tithe you are looking at that item and saying "YOU ARE NOT GOD—AND I SERVE GOD!"

Ultimately, God doesn't need just 10% of anything from us. It's all His! And when we present what is already His, He will bring more into our lives.

This is the secret to a life of freedom: you are not in charge, you are the subject of your King. In America, we don't like that concept. We would rather live our lives by our own choices, beliefs, and standards. The idea of being subject to a monarch is anathema to us. Temporally, this is a good attitude to have, but remember we are to "recognize no one according to the flesh" and that includes ourselves. Don't focus on the life you are living in the flesh as your destiny.

You see, in any earthly kingdom, all of the subjects, lands, and possessions of the realm ultimately belong to the king, but also the final responsibility for any matter rests on him. This is no less true in God's Kingdom. So when you place yourself under the subjection and care of the one true King, the balance of worry and care shifts greatly.

For example, if the King owns your house, and the house needs a new roof, then whose job is it to provide one? If you've lost your job, whose responsibility is it to help you find new employment? If you're sick, whose responsibility is it to see to it that you get healed? It is the King's!

Being A Re-Birther

Despite the authority Rabbi Jesus commanded, the plainness of His teachings and his popularity with the people, the crazy Teacher was out of favor with the leaders of the church. He simply didn't fit in with their notion of what the church should be. It would be a kind of social suicide to be seen having a conversation with the Teacher much less being overheard, agreeing with His work and worth. So, in the dark covering of night, Nicodemus, a Pharisee and member of the Sanhedrin, approached the Rabbi.

If you've read God's Word, you know the story. You know the conversation. One of the primary terms for salvation comes from the dialogue recorded in John 3:1-21. Jesus ushered in a wave of change when He uttered the words, "Most assuredly, I say to you, unless one is born again, he cannot see the kingdom of God."

Think of it! The new birth means you now see the Kingdom. Make no mistake, this is a vital aspect of understanding the mystery of the One New Man! Please don't read any of this as down-playing the importance of being born again. That re-birth is the first step in living the life God has always intended for you, but it is not the end. (We will discuss the full implication of this story later on.)

Time and space do not leave much room to discuss the element of Holy Spirit baptism that is evident in John 3, but suffice to say that, even if it were not present, the totality of Scripture plainly shows us how important it is to receive this special gift from God.

When you are baptized in the Holy Spirit you start speaking the Kingdom language and operating in its supernatural power, but you can still have the mentality that the Kingdom is "out there" somewhere. Please don't let that happen! Luke 17:21 says "the Kingdom of God is within you!" That's why you can "lay hands on the sick and they will recover," "you cast out demons," you "speak to those mountains and they move."

Most people want just enough of Jesus to keep them out of Hell, and then a little extra when they're in a bind. I promise you this: you want all of Jesus; because when you get all of Him, you receive all of everything He has. And you don't serve Him because of what He possesses, but because of Who He is. Here is the great circle: when you truly want Jesus for Who He is, you receive ALL of Who He is, which makes you love Him all the more for Who He is.

For too many, their whole world consists of eating, drinking, and worry. The Kingdom of God is not these things: it is righteousness, peace, and joy in the Holy Spirit. Why am I not anxious about the economy? Because I don't live by the economic system of the United States of America—or any other nation. I live in the economy where the King owns it all and He's never broke!

I have never seen the righteous forsaken! My God owns the cattle on a thousand hills, and He owns the hills! Why should I be worried?

In Jesus, I have *shalom*—the peace where there is nothing broken, nothing missing. Christ gives me the joy that makes me able to walk through the valley of the shadow of death.

You've Been Adopted For A Reason

Remember Tomas Martinez? There is still no word

or update on the state of his inheritance. Imagine! Six million dollars is sitting in a bank (collecting interest, by the way) and waiting for him. All he has to do is claim it.

The Kingdom of God is more than just your identity; it is your inheritance. I think that we often misunderstand this word "inheritance." Popularly and legally, the word has come to mean something you get when a person who came before you (usually in your family lineage) dies, but the idea of an inheritance is so much deeper.

When a parent passes on, for example, the child receives money, lands, property, etc., but also is now the beneficiary of all that the parent was. The legacy of the parent is passed on to the child.

The Bible teaches us that when we accept Christ, we are grafted into the lineage of Abraham. Therefore, the promises God made to Abraham are part of our inheritance. But beyond that, being connected to the Kingdom enables our influence. It isn't simply a command from God to love our neighbor's as we love ourselves, or to feed and clothe the sick; it is a privilege. We get to be, right now here on earth, the hands and feet of Jesus!

Why has God prepared a way for us to do this? Paul explains in his letter to the Ephesians that Jesus died to:

"...reconcile them both [Jew and Gentile] to God in one body through the cross, thereby

putting to death the enmity (Ephesians 2:16)
*...to the intent that NOW the manifold wisdom
of God might be made known by the CHURCH
to principalities and powers in the heavenly
places"* (3:16).

When you see Jew and Gentile uniting together in
Christ, then the *now* manifold wisdom of God,
through the church puts every devil in his place. If you
think you can get out from underneath the church and
do something for God, you're going to fail. Because
when you move from the church you are no longer
under authority.

The body of Christ was instituted for a reason,
because through it God puts every principality and
power in its rightful place.

CHAPTER 5

COMPLETELY ON PURPOSE

*Many persons have a wrong idea of
what constitutes true happiness. It is not
attained through self-gratification but
through fidelity to a worthy purpose.* [xi]
— HELEN KELLER

The story is told of an old woodcutter who, hoping to pass onto his grandson the love he had for his craft and for the nature which provided his materials, journeyed into the forest with the young boy. It would be the lad's first experience with selecting and cutting the sturdy oaks his grandfather used for the wood he would later sell to boat builders.

As they walked the half-trails of the forest, the gifted woodcutter explained to his grandson that the purpose of each tree is encompassed in its natural figure: while some are straight and make for good planks, some have the proper curvature for a boat's ribs, while yet others are tall and strong enough to be masts. He further explained that by paying attention to the details of each tree, and with gained experience in recognizing these characteristics, the young boy could, himself, become a master woodcutter.

As they walked through the forest, the grandson spotted an old oak that had never been cut, but was not very impressive in any way. It had a short and gnarled trunk and none of the limbs were straight. The boy asked if they should even bother cutting down the tree as it didn't seem good for anything but firewood. The grandfather didn't respond to the question, but instead told his grandchild that they should continue their business.

After a few hours of felling huge trees, the boy grew tired and asked if they could stop for a rest in the cool shade. The woodcutter took his grandson over to the twisted, old oak tree, and they sat against its trunk in the cool grass beneath its misshapen limbs.

After resting awhile, the old man explained to his grandson the necessity of being attentive and aware of everything in the forest and in the world.

"Some things are readily apparent," he said, "like the tall, straight trees; other things are less apparent, requiring closer attention. And some things might appear at first to have no purpose at all, like this knotted oak tree. For it is this old oak, which you so quickly assumed was useless except for firewood, that now allows us to rest against its trunk under the coolness of its shade. You must learn to pay careful attention every day so you can recognize and discover the purpose God has for everything in His creation.

THE MYSTERY OF THE ONE NEW MAN

This is true whether you are looking at trees or even if you are looking at yourself."

What timeless advice! We live in a world full of people striving to find purpose. Rick Warren has made a colossal impact on the Church and the world with his "Purpose Driven" series. It is because people everywhere desire purpose more than almost anything else. We want our lives to have meaning. We long to have our time on this earth matter.

What strikes me so cruelly is watching God-fearing, God-loving, Bible-hungry children of the Most High ignore the purpose that has been laid out for them because it does not fit comfortably inside the box of their tradition and denominational upbringing. These men and women will come to church hungry every week and ignore what God has set before them: the Mystery of the One New Man.

The purpose of the One New Man is a simple one to tell but a difficult one to grasp. In Ephesians 2:13-15, Paul revealed:

"But now in Christ Jesus you who once were far off having been brought near by the blood of Christ. For He Himself is our peace, who has made both one, and has broken down the middle wall of separation. Having abolished in His flesh the enmity, that is, the law of the commandments contained in ordinances, so as to create in Himself ONE NEW MAN from the two, thus making peace."

51

Please take note of a few things here. First, the phrase "you who were far off." This isn't about geography. It speaks instead to the degree of separation from the promises and blessings of Abraham faced by us Gentiles. We were separated from the story of Covenant. The Good News is that because of the blood of Jesus we have "been brought near" to those promises. They are accessible to us now.

Next, observe this phrase: "having abolished in His flesh the enmity..." Sin creates that anger, wrath, murder, and the spirit of death in us. Jesus abolished that enmity in HIS flesh. It was in us because there were commandments and ordinances that we could not keep. And the anger and frustration of not being able to live up to a religious requirement made people angry, but Jesus took away the hatred and nailed it to the cross.

Finally, see that through this process Christ has created "in Himself One New Man *from the two*, thus making peace." God has erased the line of demarcation between Jew and Gentile and created instead, the One New Man: the Christian.

This isn't a statement of declaration that the Church has replaced Israel. It is absolutely not an affirmation of replacement theology. However, the Bible clearly shows that this creation of the One New Man has happened intentionally on God's part. How did it happen?

It's important to understand that God made a

covenant with Adam in the Garden of Eden. The first man was placed in a perfect paradise. Remember, he was given authority, power, and dominion over the earth even down to naming the animals. Then sin entered. Death came into the world through Adam's fall. In this, Adam forefeited what was his.

Centuries later, God called Abram out of Ur which is in modern-day Iraq. Ur was an ancient capital, and archaeology reveals a city of approximately 360,000 people. Further discoveries have shown that Ur was a city devoted to idol worship. Jewish tradition states that Abram's father, Terah, was a maker of idols. But, when God called Abram out of Ur, He made a series of covenant promises.

God promised to make Abram's descendants a mighty nation, to bless Abram materially and make his name great, and to protect Abram by blessing those who blessed him, and cursing all who opposed him.

So, you see that God was establishing a father of a new nation, and that Covenant Nation was to deliver the return of all that Adam forfeited; the restoration of God's Kingdom. This nation failed to receive what the Lord had promised, and outright rejected the bearer of that Kingdom, Jesus Christ. (Don't be concerned; none of this was a surprise to God.)

So the Almighty turned to "strangers from the covenants of promise," and "aliens from the commonwealth of Israel" who had "no hope and [were] without God in the world." By doing this, Jesus abolished the enmity, took away the separation and

53

made in Himself the One New Man.

So now we understand how it happened, but the better question is, "Why did God do it this way?"

Exceeding Riches

In the past few years, there has been seemingly endless discussion on the economy. Bailouts, spending, deficit, debt, loans, salaries, and taxes... Oh my, indeed! I sometimes wonder at the amounts mentioned. Numbers like, million, billion, and trillion are tossed around as freely as you or I would tens or hundreds. It's hard to imagine these numbers. Let's take a moment to look at some comparisons.

The median annual salary in the United States is $26,197. In contrast, when Paula Abdul was a celebrity judge on *The X Factor*, she was paid $2.5 million, Hugh Laurie, the star of *House*, made $16.8 million, Charlie Sheen raked in $28.8 million, while Simon Cowell, a record executive and entrepreneur, garnered a stunning $75 million.

There is a fun, if somewhat sobering, tool available on the website: bankrate.com. It compares celebrity salaries to the U.S. average in a "rubber meets the road" fashion. For example, if the purchase price of your house was $252,000, to the actor Robert Downey Jr., that house would have seemed to cost $213. That $600 laptop you purchased would have seemed to film star Adam Sandler like $0.41. The hotel room that you paid $130 for would have cost

Brad Pitt a stunning $0.17. Your new iPhone with 64GB Hard Drive that cost $400 would have set Johnny Depp back $0.21. If you decided to really splurge and buy yourself a brand new Bentley Continental Supersports Coupe, you would have been hit in the pocket book for a whopping $275,000. Will Smith would have paid, in comparison, less than $200.

But these are just "celebrity" salaries. Consider other well-known businessmen and entrepreneurs. Mark Zuckerberg, the inventor of Facebook became worth $17.5 billion. Software billionaire Larry Ellison is one of the richest men in America. By 2011, he had accumulated a net worth of $27 billion. This sum is enough to allow him to spend about $51 million per week—or $303,000 every hour—without ever touching his principal.

Think about some of the governmental spending that's occurred over the last few years. CitiBank, deemed "too big to fail," received a federal bailout in the sum of $345 billion. Social Security programs cost $731 billion. Obamacare is expected to cost $1.76 trillion.

When analysts, pundits, and other talking-heads mention these sums, we tend to become immune to the enormity of it all. Let's take a moment to put some numbers in perspective. Consider the size of our dollars. At just over 2.5 inches tall and six inches wide, our paper money is easily carried in a pocket, wallet, or change purse, even at our largest denominations.

Now consider the $100 bill. Most everyone has seen or even held one of these at some point. A standard bank stack of them, totaling $10,000, is less than ½" thick. This size allows for $1,000,000, or 100 $10,000 stacks, to be easily placed inside of a plastic grocery bag. It seems paradoxical that so much money could be placed in so small a container.

Consider $100,000,000 in the same stacks. That money would require a standard military pallet (35"x45.5") and be less than four feet high. One person could move that around with just a hand truck. But what about $1 Billion ($1,000,000,000 or 100,000 stacks of the aforementioned $10,000 stacks)? That would require 10 standard military pallets. Now let's go for some really big dollars.

How much room would one need to house $1 trillion ($1,000,000,000)? Remember the standard military pallets? One would have to double stack the pallets and then place them in a space equivalent to the length and width of a standard American Football field. Take a moment to let that image sink in. That's approximately 8 feet high, 360 feet long, and 160 feet wide in $100 bills.

Can you imagine that much money? You or I might not be able to visualize having even one pallet of $100 bills, much less the 1,000 pallets required to achieve $1 trillion! Still, it's a little easier to conceive of the amount when we are able to put it in some kind of spatial perspective. But why have I spent all of this space talking about money?

This is not the place to go into tithing principles or applications, but God knows that we have a tendency to place a great deal of faith in temporal, worldly wealth. That's one of the reasons, I think, that Jesus talked more about money than He did Heaven and Hell combined. In fact, Jesus spoke more on this topic than He did anything else except the Kingdom of God. He wanted us to have a proper understanding and appreciation of our worldly treasures. We do not trust in silver or gold (or pallets of $100 bills). We place our trust in God. How are we able to do that?

Paul said in Ephesians 2, God let history play out this way so that, "in the ages to come He might show the exceeding riches of His grace in His kindness toward us in Christ Jesus."

God did it all so that we might see the "unfathomable riches" found in Christ. Yes, $1 trillion dollars is a lot of money, and while we may never own it, we can at least now comprehend the magnitude of that amount. But the Bible says that God has "exceeding riches" of grace and that they are "unfathomable." We cannot even begin to grasp the enormity of the length, width, and breadth of God's grace toward us in Christ Jesus.

Understand what this word "exceeding" means. The standard dictionary definition is "exceptional in amount, quality, or degree," but that doesn't really convey the Greek understanding of this word.

There is, inherent in the term, the idea of meeting a need in a way that is far beyond what is required to get the job done. Imagine it this way: It's game seven of the World Series. It is the bottom of the 9th and the score is tied. The bases are loaded as you step to the plate. Swing and a miss! Strike one! Then ball one and ball two. Oh no! That curve ball caught you looking! Strike two! Here it comes… NO! That one is far too inside. Ball three! Now it's crunch time.

The count it full. Whatever happens this next pitch will decide the World Series. But come on… All you need is a base hit to make it happen. If one runner gets to home plate, your team wins. You psych yourself up for it as you return to the batter's box.

The pitcher winds up and everything synchronizes; the wind dies down, the crowd becomes amazingly silent to you, and the ball appears to be coming at you in slow motion. It's a fastball right in your zone.

You squeeze the bat, shift your weight back and then forward as you tear into the ball. The resounding crack echoes throughout the stadium. You look up to see the ball forming a perfect arc that takes it not just past the baseline, not simply into lower outfield, not to the outer edges of the field, not even into the stands, but far, far out of the stadium and into the parking lot. Goodbye, Mr. Spalding! More than the required base hit, you have tattooed that ball into baseball history.

God's exceeding riches are like that! It's far greater than you can imagine, because it's so much more than is needed.

In the Jewish Passover, there is a song called the Dayenu. It is a song meant to teach the order of events in Jewish history, but also to express thanks for all that God has done. The word means "it would have been enough for us." It has fifteen short stanzas, at the end of each the word "Dayenu" is sung. They sing:

If He had only brought us out of Egypt –
Dayenu!
If He had only executed justice on the
Egyptians – Dayenu!
If He had only executed justice upon their
gods – Dayenu!
If He had only slain their first born – Dayenu!
If He had only given to us their health and
wealth – Dayenu!
If He had only split the sea for us – Dayenu!
If He had only led us through on dry land –
Dayenu!
If He had only drowned our oppressors –
Dayenu!
If He had only provided for our needs in the
wilderness for only forty years – Dayenu!
If He had only fed us manna – Dayenu!
If He had only given us Sabbath – Dayenu!
If He had only led us to Mount Sinai –
Dayenu!
If He had only given us the Torah – Dayenu!
If He had only brought us into the Land of
Israel – Dayenu!
If He had only built the Temple for us –
Dayenu!

Yes, it would have been enough! But God is not a God of "enough." He had so much more in store for the children of Israel and for all of mankind. God had in mind, before the foundation of the world, that Christ's sacrifice would be a demonstration of the great riches of the depth and breadth of His grace toward us.

Jesus didn't do *just enough* for us. He went overboard to give us an overload of His overabundant grace and spiritual riches. Look at how Paul describes the situation in Ephesians 1:3 he says that God has blessed us "with every spiritual blessing in the heavenly places in Christ."

Not some spiritual blessings, but *every* spiritual blessing! In verse 4, he reminds us, "God chose us in Him before the foundation of the world." Try to wrap your mind around that!

Before He ever uttered the words "Let there be," He knew you, called you, set you apart and wrote your name in The Book of Life.

Ages to Come

Finally, it is important to take note of the phrase, "ages to come." This does not, as some teach, refer to when the Church finds herself in Heaven; it means right now! Currently, the earth rests in the middle of the Church Age, the Age of the Gentiles. The Age of the Jew, which will fulfill the covenant, is yet to come. To be true to context, it is in the dispensation of grace that we live now, but when we leave, there will be seven years grafted back into time that allows the Jews to be the evangelistic tool on this earth.

In the meantime, God is revealing through us the exceeding riches of His grace so that, according to Romans 9, 10, and 11, in the ages to come, it will cause the Jews to become "jealous of us." Through the One New Man, God will show the Jews the exceeding wealth of His grace upon the Gentiles.

In Ephesians 1:5, Paul fearlessly brings up the touchy subject of predestination when he says that God "predestined us to adoption as sons by Jesus Christ to Himself, according to the good pleasure of His will." The word here really means that He set our destiny in order.

In verses 6 and 7, we're told that God "made us accepted in the beloved" by "redemption through His blood" which provided "the forgiveness of sins."

Because of this, we have, according to verse 11, "obtained an inheritance." What is that inheritance? Verses 13 and 14 point out that we have been given an earnest payment of that inheritance when God "sealed us with the Holy Spirit of promise" Who is the "guarantee of our inheritance until the redemption of the purchased possession."

All of this just scratches the surface of what God has in store. He has made provision for you according to His exceeding riches. Reach out and take what God has offered!

CHAPTER 6

THE MIRACLE
IN THE WATER

*Baptism was to put a line of demarcation
between your past sins when you are buried
with Him by Baptism—you are burying your
past sins—eradicating them—putting a line in
the sand saying that old man is dead and
he is no longer alive any more and I rise
up to walk in the newness of life.* [xii]

– T. D. JAKES

Baptism is faith in action. [xiii]

– WATCHMAN NEE

A friend of mine tells the story of a conversation he had with a female resident in the children's home where he and his wife were ministering as house-parents.

As she sat directly across from me, I could see in her eyes a kind of disgust with herself. I was reminded of Paul's expression of frustration "For what I am doing, I do not understand. For what I will to do, that I do not practice; but what I hate, that I do."

She was involved with a boy who had at least one other confirmed girlfriend (who was pregnant), she was constantly in trouble at school, a bane to her teachers and the administration at the home. Her parents, and all of her family had abandoned her. She never had visitors.

Yet, almost nightly when I went in for bed check I could tell she had been crying. Usually when asked why, she would brush it off and dismiss the question. One night, though, she opened up and we talked for a couple of hours about some of the choices she had made and those she seemed unable to make. In those moments of clarity, she knew what she should do and why. Her desire to "be good" was clear, but she didn't seem to know how to do it.

When I spoke to her of the power that was available to her through the Holy Spirit, her interest piqued, but she seemed to deflate when I reiterated that the choice was hers and that she would have to make some hard decisions every day. She had to decide to do the right thing. The first being to recommit her life to Christ.

After talking for a while, she said something

very unexpected; "I guess I'm gonna have to get baptized again, huh?"

I was befuddled. I scanned my memory to think of a reason someone might think this, but I could come up with nothing. "What do you mean?" I finally asked.

"Well, you know... I've sinned since the last time I got baptized, so I have to get baptized again so God will forgive me." [xiv]

Obviously, this young girl had experienced either some shoddy teaching on baptism or there had been a disconnect in her mental processing of it. Still, the veracity of baptism as a sacrament is hardly questionable. Jesus commanded His disciples to go "and make disciples of all the nations, baptizing them in the name of the Father and of the Son and of the Holy Spirit" (Matthew 28:19). So, yes, baptism is important; but why?

Take a moment and really think about this. Have you ever been baptized? Did your parents tell you it was meaningful? Did your pastor? A brother or sister in Christ? Was it ever explained to you? I've heard sincere Christians say that they were baptized because it was "an important ritual," "a rite of passage," or that it was important because "that's how God washes the last bit of sin off of you." (That person was in his 30s. I wish I was making this up.)

So, like the girl in the beginning of this chapter, there is some misunderstanding.

As with any teaching it is vital to return to the Bible and see what is written there. We've already mentioned the Great Commission found in Matthew, but there is a deep teaching found in the epistles of Paul concerning baptism that can both liberate and shock the believer.

A Watery Grave

In his great theological discourse to the church at Rome, Paul had some stirring things to say about baptism, and it is important that we break each part down and look at what it actually says, and then how it is applied in the life of the One New Man.

The sixth chapter of Romans is a litany of hard sayings that cut through all of the pretense so easily found in the life of the believer. Look at verse 2 where he asks, "how shall we who *died to sin* live any longer in it?"

Take a moment and let that sink in. Died! It's past tense. It has already happened. Here, Paul is again saying that the believer is *dead.* The believer is dead to sin. It's not simply a question of having a conscience installed in your brain, or the ability to better know the difference between right and wrong. When you accept Christ, you die to sin!

Paul follows this question with another equally confrontational when he queries in verse 3, "Or do you not know that as many of us as were baptized into Christ Jesus were baptized into His death?" Think of that! When you immersed in the waters of baptism you are baptized not into your own death but into Jesus' death!

If that were the end of it, things would be powerful enough, but look at what Paul explains to us later:

"Therefore we were buried with Him through baptism into death, that just as Christ was raised from the dead by the glory of the Father, even so we also should walk in newness of life. For if we have been united together in the likeness of His death, certainly we also shall be in the likeness of His resurrection, knowing this, that our old man was crucified with Him, that the body of sin might be done away with, that we should no longer be slaves of sin. For he who has died has been freed from sin.

Now if we died with Christ, we believe that we shall also live with Him, knowing that Christ, having been raised from the dead, dies no more. Death no longer has dominion over Him… For sin shall not have dominion over you" (Romans 6:4-9,14).

Let that promise soak into your inner man. "Sin shall not have dominion over you." Dominion is defined as "ruling control" or a "sphere of influence." Now read it like this, because of that baptism into Christ's death, "sin will not have rule, control, or even a sphere of influence over you." Why is that? Go further back into the chapter.

There are some churches which teach that our "old man" is really a dual nature. You get saved, but you have an old man and a new man and they are in constant battle with each other, but not according to Paul. The apostle says the old man has been crucified. He's dead! Why? So that the "body of sin"—in my estimation this is a body of evidence against you—"might be done away with."

This old man, who knew how to sin from the time he was in the crib, and couldn't stop doing what he did, is dead and gone!

Paul points out that, through baptism, we were connected to Jesus' death, but Jesus, though He died physically did not stay in the grave. Verses 4 and 5 tell us "we were buried with Him through baptism into death, that just as Christ was raised from the dead by the glory of the Father, even so we also [are made able to] walk in newness of life."

Though we died, we did not remain dead. In Christ, we are raised again just as He was raised. So, the miracle of our water baptism is that when Jesus died, I died. You can't even argue that you weren't born yet, because God knew you before the foundation of the world.

Before the Creator of all things ever said the first "Let there be…," He knew your name and everything about you and prepared a destiny for you to be saved and converted into the One New Man through the atoning work of Christ Jesus.

When Jesus hung on the cross, He took upon Himself every sin, every addiction, every crime, every evil and lustful thought, every loss of temper, every thorn and thistle from this earth! Jesus took it all and determined that whosoever would call on Him would be redeemed. The Creator decided before this world was even formed that all should be saved, "for God is not willing that any should perish but that all should come to repentance."

Does that mean everyone goes to Heaven and there is no Hell? Absolutely not! God has written out a destiny for every person that was ever conceived on this planet, and part of that destiny was that they come to know the grace, mercy, and all-consuming love that is found in God, but it is our choice to accept this.

If we choose not to do so, it says twice in Revelation, that person's name is blotted out of the Book of Life. Our name is not written into the Book when we get saved—every person's name was recorded before time began—but if you choose to ignore God's grace and forgiveness, you will literally go to Hell over Jesus' dead body!

In addition, when Christ was buried I was buried. It's important to understand this because everyone knows what you do with a dead body; you place it in the ground and cover it up. So many Christians go down into the waters of baptism and, when they rise up they put a hook in that old dead body and drag it around for the rest of their days? Do you want to know who these people are? Ask for their testimony. Is it filled with defeat, death, depression, addiction? Is it full of "I'm struggling" and "every day is a battle"? If so, you can probably count on the fact that if you look behind them, they've got an old "dead them" that they're dragging around!

Back in the 80s, there was a popular expression in churches that went something like this: "When the devil reminds you of your past, just remind him of his future." That sounds fine and good, but it misses the point. You see, if the devil shows up to remind you of your past, why aren't you telling him, "I don't know who you're talking about, because that person is dead and has been for a long time! I put him in the grave and he's still there! If you have a problem with me, take it up with Jesus, because He is the only person inside me!" It really is that simple.

Finally, remember that if He was raised, then so are you! According to the Bible, you are with Him in Heaven, right now! You are already seated in Heavenly places with God's Son.

One of the biggest lies the devil ever sold the Church was that you have to hang on, hold on, pray through, keep the law, tow the line, ride the rules or you might lose your salvation as easily as you lose your wallet! Let me remind you that you didn't do anything to earn your salvation, you don't have to do anything to hold onto it, and you can't do anything to lose it! You're already in Heaven! How can you die and go to Hell if you're already residing in Heaven?

I can hear some of you now, "Pastor Dwain, that's

just the old Baptist doctrine 'once saved always saved' that you learned growing up." No, it most certainly is not. This is the eternal security of the believer. You can't just join a church, get wet and keep living like Hell and be saved. If you do, your old man is not dead. If your old man is truly dead, then he has been crucified and buried and a new you has been raised up. You have been made *kainos* (brand new) in the eyes of God. Why are you not that way in your own eyes?

The Water Speaks

Romans 6 isn't the only place that Paul teaches about baptism. In the letter to the Colossians, Paul likens baptism to circumcision. He says in chapter 2 verse 11, "In Him you were also circumcised with the circumcision made without hands, by putting off the body of the sins of the flesh, by the circumcision of Christ."

Examine the phrase, "The circumcision of Christ." What does that mean? Is there a clue elsewhere in the verse? Think about the words, "circumcision made without hands." This points out that what Paul speaks of here is a spiritual circumcision. So, Christ was spiritually circumcised.

Paul continues the idea of us "putting off the body of the sins of the flesh, by the circumcision of Christ" by saying that we have been "buried with Him in baptism, in which you were also raised with Him through faith in the working of God, who raised Him from the dead" (Colossians 2:12). Why is this circumcision so significant?

Thousands of years before Christ's death, burial, and resurrection, the patriarch Abram was given a promise that would extend to his seed. The word was singular because the Seed is Christ Jesus. Remember how God accomplished this.

Abram had been promised he would be the father of a new nation, and that his descendants would outnumber the sands of the shore and the stars in the sky. But here he was, a hundred years old and far past the ability to give children to his wife Sarai, who was herself way past childbearing years. He was "over the hill," until God circumcised him. I'm not talking about the removal of his foreskin. I am referring to God reaching into Abram's body and cutting away the deadness!

God circumcised him and something miraculous happened. His name had to be changed from Abram to Abraham. This is worth noting if you like to understand Hebrew. There is a word in Hebrew, "ruach." It means breath. When God changed Abram's name it was because God Himself breathed new life into that old man. Abraham was baptized in the Holy Ghost, the Seed of God entered his body and the promise was given.

One of the most glorious things I've ever seen is when a person goes down into the waters of baptism, comes up, and while still dripping wet receives the baptism of the Holy Ghost. This happened all the time in the New Testament, and it gets me excited when it takes place today!

Let's refer back to Colossians. In verse 13 Paul says, "And you, being dead in your trespasses and the uncircumcision of your flesh, He has made alive together with Him, having forgiven you all trespasses" (Colossians 2:13).

Prior to salvation, we are uncircumcised, but the process of salvation is our circumcision, and when that happens Paul goes on to say that it "wipe[s] out the handwriting of requirements that was against us, which was contrary to us. And [Jesus] has taken it out of the way, having nailed it to the cross" (Colossians 2:13-14).

Our old nature, that uncircumcised dead part of us, has been nailed to the cross by the only One to ever defeat the power of the cross, death, Hell, and the grave!

In doing this, Jesus, "disarmed principalities and powers, He made a public spectacle of them, triumphing over them in it." If you feel like the devil is attacking you, latch onto this promise. It isn't merely that no weapon formed against you will prosper, it's that every weapon that was ever formed that might be used against you has already been destroyed by the power of Jesus. When He did this He made a laughing stock of those who would attack.

Why do we fear the powers of Hell when we are supposed to be laughing at their defeat? Why do we walk around biting our spiritual fingernails and knocking our knees together out of fear that the enemy is going to send some demon to try and oppress us when Jesus has already triumphed over them?

One of my favorite television shows is the old Andy Griffith sitcom. Everything about that series was great, especially Don Knotts. He had a comedic timing and ability to mug for the camera that was second to none.

I remember an episode where his character Barney was without his trusty six-shooter (or the single bullet he kept in his shirt pocket) and he had to thwart some thugs. So he decided to stick his hand in his pocket and pretend to have a gun. Of course the thugs caught on, and weren't at all afraid of him.

This is exactly how we need to react when we feel Satan trying to mount an attack. Just picture him as a bumbling fool who is without a weapon of any kind. See him sticking his hand in his coat pocket so you'll think he's a threat. And then, in the name of Jesus, you rebuke and remind him that he's not only already a defeated foe, but he is, in fact, a colossal joke that deserves no more of your energy than it takes to laugh at him. Call him out for the loser that Jesus made him!

Satan has been disarmed. The *only* way he can bother you is if you believe his lies.

The point is, when you go into the watery grave of baptism, you are given the power to do these same things. Your death, burial, and resurrection, because of Jesus, makes a mockery of Satan, completely disarms him, and makes him a laughing stock for all of creation to see. And yet, so many Christians walk around acting defeated, allowing Satan to dredge up their past, causing them to live in shame.

The message of baptism is that you have been given the power to put Satan in his place; defeated and drowning, clinging to that old dead body you left back in the water.

Mysteries In The Deep

I believe in deliverance ministries, but I am also convinced that the Church wouldn't even need deliverance ministries if people could grasp the revelation of baptism the first time. Why is it so difficult? It is because there is a mysterious element to baptism and it is connected intrinsically and indelibly to the mystery of the One New Man.

Look back at Ephesians 2. Here again Paul brings up the circumcision aspect of this process. He does so by admonishing us to remember that "you, once Gentiles in the flesh..."

I absolutely love the word "once." That little word says "here's what used to be but is no more and can't be again." That packs a lot of punch for a tiny four-letter word. Paul tells us that we were "once Gentiles in the flesh." Well, if we were *once* that, what are we now? Get ready for this!

If you are a believer in Christ, and you have been baptized in this method, you're a Jew. I will never understand why people are so bothered by this simple truth. John the Baptist said to the Pharisees, "Do not presume to say to yourselves, 'We are children of Abraham,' for I tell you that God can raise up children of Abraham from these very stones!" And that's just what God did. When the Jewish people—"He came to His own, and His own did not receive Him" (John 1:11)—rejected Jesus (again, God was not surprised by this), they renounced their right to the promises of Abraham. The Gentiles were strangers and aliens not only to the land of Israel but to all of the promises of Abraham. But because of Jesus, we have been "brought near" (Ephesians 2:13) and made new.

Jesus has broken down the middle wall of separation by fulfilling the law for you. This produced peace between God and man, and, in doing this, He has reconciled Jew and Gentile in Himself, making One New Man from the two, and putting to death the enmity that once existed between you and God and has replaced it with His perfect agape love.

Do you have to be baptized? No. The thief on the cross is proof of that. But the waters of baptism are where you publicly confess Jesus, who said if you deny Me before men, I will deny you before My Father.

The point is that, in the history of the New Testament, there is not even a hint that a new believer would have accepted Jesus and not had an urgent desire to be baptized. Such a thing wouldn't even have crossed their minds. This is because just as physical circumcision is the physical mark of the covenant made with Abraham, baptism is the spiritual mark of your covenant with the One who fulfilled all of those promises made to Abraham: Jesus. The One New Man is received at salvation, but it is restored at baptism.

Baptism Now

In recent months, I have seen over 5,000 baptized into the One New Man. Some of these are being immersed for the first time as a confession of their faith in Jesus Christ. While for others it is their second immersion into the One New Man revelation. I believe this revelation is a trustworthy teaching. Water baptism is essential to clarify your true identity in Christ and receiving your inheritance as the "seed" of Abraham.

Remember the story of Zechariah and his wife Elizabeth who was with child. An angel came and told him that the child's name was to be John. Why? He should have been named Zechariah. He should have been the High Priest of Israel. God closed Zechariah's mouth just in case he had another idea about naming the boy. Certainly God wanted this child to be part of the priesthood of Israel, but the priesthood had become corrupt. They were selling God's forgiveness at the Temple, twisting and distorting the law so that it fit and served their selfish purposes. So the Lord called John out of that corruption, and sent him to live among the Essenes—an ultra-ritualistic Jewish sect.

In the Essene communities there were many mitvahs or baptismal pools. These people were, for lack of a better word, rather different. They were eagerly awaiting the arrival of Messiah, and they believed that He would be a *spiritual* Messiah. They would bathe themselves three times a day, all the while calling out for the Promised One to appear.

When the time was right, God sent John, who Jesus called "that Elijah which was to come," as the high priest who would call the people to repent, but who would also prepare the way for the Messiah Himself.

When John baptized Jesus, he was baptizing Him into the priesthood. You see God had rejected one order of priesthood and instituted, first in John, a new one. Not the Aaronic priesthood that had become so depraved, but into the priesthood of Melchizidek whom Abraham had met in a theophany, or visit from God. Melchizidek was Christ in the Old Testament.

There, in the cold waters of the Jordan, Jesus fulfilled what Abraham had seen. He became your High Priest. When you get baptized, you not only confess Jesus, you declare that God has made you a priest and king as well. You are a living fulfillment of a four-thousand-year-old promise! How can you ever fail?

Back to Ephesians

There is a great Hebrew word that we all horribly dilute. The word is *shalom*. Everyone thinks it just means "peace," and that is a perfectly fine translation. However, at a deeper level, the word means "nothing broken—nothing missing."

In Ephesians 2 we see a wonderful promise:

"For He Himself is our peace, who has made both one, and has broken down the middle wall of separation, having abolished in His flesh the enmity, that is, the law of commandments contained in ordinances, so as to create in Himself one new man from the two, thus making peace" (Ephesians 2:14-15).

It's incredible to know that our peace doesn't derive from circumstances or situations, but that when we have Jesus, we have perfect peace because He is everything we need. Some people think that when we talk about the Baptism of the Holy Spirit, we are actually saying that there is more of God you need or have to get. This isn't the case at all. But in yourself, unless you learn to release all that you have, you will never operate in fullness.

Most Christians are functioning either in their soul or their flesh without understanding that there is a spiritual DNA that—if it can break through the barrier of your flesh and your soul—can bring the DNA of the Creator Himself through you in signs, wonders and miracles!

Again, remember that the middle wall of separation prevented Gentiles from being saved. This was erased when Jesus abolished, in His flesh, the enmity between God and man.

CHAPTER 7

ELEPHANTS
AND FLOWERS

*Wise leaders should have known that
the human heart cannot exist in a vacuum.
If Christians are forbidden to enjoy the wine
of the Spirit they will turn to the wine of the
flesh....Christ died for our hearts and the Holy
Spirit wants to come and satisfy them.* [xv]

— A. W. TOZER

Actor and comedian Russell Brand tells a funny story about meeting with an executive at MTV in preparation for his hosting duties at the 2008 MTV Video Music Awards.

The executives were bringing Brand up to speed on the promotional plans for the show. For one of the commercials, Brand was to sit on a couch and just have a conversation with Britney Spears. In case you don't follow popular culture, 2007 was certainly not a great year for Britney. There were breakdowns, head shavings, horrid paparazzi photo moments; the list is terrifying.

Brand asked the executives, who were promoting him as "edgy," if he planned to say something sarcastic to her. He acknowledged that Spears had been through a tough year, but he didn't really feel comfortable talking about her problems.

He explained his position, saying, "I don't want to talk about it, but it's going to be difficult not to... Don't you think there's going to be kind of an elephant in the room?" Brand tells what happened next:

> *The MTV executive to his eternal credit said, "What if there literally was an elephant in the room?"*

And what that comment created is what is now considered one of the great popular culture commercial landmarks. Brand and Spears sit and talk about nothing while an elephant literally walks through the room. The episode drew critical and professional praise as well as serving as the launch point for Britney Spears' second career wind. [xvi]

There is, among Christians, a kind of elephant in the room. It's not the traditional pachyderm that no one wants to talk about. In truth, there seems to be no end to dialogue, discussion, debate, and dueling over this issue, but that only happens when people move past the elephant stage.

I've seen it in teenagers and pensioners, in the

affluent and poor, in conservative and liberal, in every denomination and subset in the Universal Church. Whenever two Christians meet, the elephant in the room always seems to be: "What do you think about the Baptism of the Holy Spirit?"

You've got cessationists and continuationists, hardline Pentecostals, ultra-conservative Baptists, charismatic Methodists, Glosso-Yalies, people who wouldn't fall down if you prayed over them with a sledgehammer and those who will get slain in the Spirit if the wind blows too hard. It is a smorgasbord of differences.

But the one thing that no Christian can do with the Baptism of the Holy Spirit is leave it alone. Whatever you believe, and wherever you decide to land on the subject, no Christian can just be Switzerland and stay completely neutral. Every denomination, whatever they tend to believe, tends to have a very different viewpoint.

I share my thoughts on this subject here, because I believe that understanding the topics discussed in this book are vital to comprehending the mystery of the One New Man and, consequently, fundamental to you living the kind of Christian life that God has always intended for you.

If you come from a denominational background that says you receive the Baptism of the Holy Spirit when you get saved, then you are being totally and intentionally inconsistent with the Greek language of the New Testament.

There is no way a person can believe that the Baptism of the Holy Spirit completely and totally happened when you were born again. When you are saved you do get all of Jesus, and thank God for that. But the Bible is clear that in the life of a believer there is a second experience that launches that individual into everything that Christ is. You have all of Jesus, but with the Baptism of the Holy Spirit, Jesus is getting all of you. Even that doesn't fully convey the power of this divine experience.

The Pentecostal world has, by and large, relegated the Baptism of the Holy Spirit to speaking in tongues. You might have heard it before. It's part of a question that they all tend to ask. It is never enough that you're saved. It's not even enough that you've received the Baptism of the Holy Spirit. They want to know "Have-you-been- saved-sanctified-delievered-and-filled-with-the-Holy-Ghost-with-the- initial-evidence-of-speaking-in-other-tongues-as-the-Holy-Spirit-gave-you-utterance?" I mean it's a brainful to take in!

In doing this they have stolen the magnitude and the power of the Baptism of the Holy Spirit from the Church. Tongues is a tiny portion of the Baptism in the Holy Spirit. So, if you tend to get caught on either side of the tongues part of this experience, just wait. There is so much more for you.

You see, if the receiving of the One New Man happens through the crucified life, and the revelation of the One New Man happens through the demonstration of the riches of God's grace, and the One New

Man is restored through water baptism, it is important to understand that the One New Man is released into operation and inheritance through the Baptism of the Holy Spirit.

I am totally convinced that if you, as a child of God and follower of Jesus Christ, want to thrive and not just survive in these last days, then you must be baptized in the Holy Spirit. It is the power of God for the Christian life!

I acknowledge that this is a controversial subject. I grew up in a denomination that had left its roots and stopped believing in the Baptism of the Holy Spirit altogether. Some people think that the Baptist world never believed in this experience, and that is simply not true. We didn't stop embracing it until the turn of the 20th Century. To understand this, let's take a brief look at some church history.

A Brief History Lesson

Some teachers say that all Protestants came out of a church system that was rooted in Rome. That is absolutely not true. Many orthodox believers did, but not all. It must be understood that there was a Great Schism that happened long ago. One branch was called the Eastern Church and one was called the Roman church. The problem is that not all of the Eastern Church was in the East. Branches such as Anabaptists, Waldenses, Moravians, Coptics, etc., all are linked to the Eastern Orthodox Church.

The reason this is significant is because when Luther brought about the Reformation, there was a revolt against his teachings because many did not accept sprinkling or infant baptism. These people were, essentially, rebels to the Reformation. Let me give you one short story to illustrate how violent this demarcation was.

In 1525, in the town of Freiberg, Germany, a Benedictine monk by the name of Michael Sattler, impressed and motivated by a peasant protest at St. Peter's monastery, left his order. Sattler married a former nun by the name of Margaretha, and in the face of growing persecution, they fled to Zurich where Felix Manz, Conrad Grebel, and Georg Blaurock were in the midst of a split from Ulrich Zwingli. All of them were banished from Zurich in late 1525.

In less than a year, Sattler had gone from loyal, celibate Benedictine monk to loyal, married, exiled "heretic" embracing the Anabaptist faith.

Sattler was the primary author of the Schleitheim Confession, one of the most important documents in Anabaptist, and Church, history. Essentially, the confession affirmed that baptism was to be administered only to those who made a conscious act of repentance and have affirmed a belief in the work of Christ via His atoning death on the cross.

Most importantly, and in direct contradiction to existing church practices, infants were not to be baptized. Additionally, the sacrament of communion was made available only to those believers who had made the aforementioned conscious decisions of repentance and been baptized.

The confession also showed the earliest signs of the seedling that would become, centuries later, the Holiness movement. It affirmed that the body of believers should completely disassociate, as much as they were able, with any who had strayed from the faith or renounced God and lived in rebellion against Him.

With the other articles contained within, The Schleitheim Confession was to become foundational to the Anabaptists and its popularity caused Ulrich Zwingli to write a response, "Refutation of Anabaptist Tricks."

Now on the run from two fronts in Christendom, the Sattlers, along with other Anabaptists, were eventually caught and arrested by Roman Catholic authorities. Sattler himself was charged:

- That he and his adherents have acted contrary to the mandate of the Emperor.
- He has taught, held, and believed that the body and blood of Christ are not present in the sacrament.
- He has taught and believed that infant baptism does not conduce to salvation.
- They have rejected the sacrament of extreme unction.

- They have despised and condemned the mother of God and the saints.
- He has declared that men are not to swear before the authorities.
- He has commenced a new and unheard of custom in regard to the Lord's Supper, placing the bread and wine on a plate, and eating and drinking the same.
- He has left the order, and married a wife.
- He has said that if the Turks should invade the country, no resistance ought to be offered them; and if it were right to wage war, he would rather take the field against the Christians than against the Turks; and it is certainly a great matter, to set the greatest enemies of our holy faith against us.

After a zealous interrogation by the Town Clerk, Sattler was sentenced. For his crimes, many and heinous as they plainly were to the authorities, Michael Sattler was sentenced to have his tongue cut out, his skin torn seven times with hot tongs and to then be burned at the stake.

His wife and others had a less grisly fate. They were, for their crimes of defying the only "true Mother Church," bound at their hands and feet, made to squat down so as to allow a rod to be placed at the crook of their knees and elbows. They were then taken to the middle of a river and, in a mockery of their practice of adult baptism, plunged repeatedly into the water until drowned; a death by baptism. [xvii]

My friend Ron Phillips was in Bethlehem during the Eastern Orthodox celebration of Christmas, which happens in January. An intifada had been declared and, though most tour groups had wisely left the country, Ron and his folks decided to stay. This service is one of the highest of the High Holy days in that church. They stood in what should have been standing-room-only circumstances in the Church of the Nativity. Ron tells this story:

> As the priests were going through their rituals, lighting incense and chanting, all of a sudden a Holy Ghost teardown broke out and these priests started speaking in tongues, crying and falling on their faces before God. Heaven opened up and the glory of God fell down right in the middle of that Greek church.
>
> This High Priest there, stood up in a vestment that was over 700 years old and began to read Scripture and quote spiritual things. You could just tell that God had manifested Himself in a fresh way in that place. After the service was over, I went over to the man and spoke with him.
>
> I found out he came from Syria and was a member of a group of 5,000 Syrian Christians who still speak the same Aramaic that Jesus spoke 2,000 years ago. They trace their heritage all the way back to the same shore of Galilee

that Jesus walked and preached from. The man asked me, "What are you?" "I'm a Baptist," I replied.

The High Priest said, "So am I. You see we immerse three times. Backwards twice, 'In the name of the Father, and in the name of the Son' and then we baptize forward, 'in the name of the Holy Ghost.' And then we take the holy anointing oil and pour it all over the person saying 'Now may you be baptized with the charisma, which is the gift of the Holy Spirit."

That's the heritage of Baptists and Pentecostals.

Why is any of this significant? Because we live in a time when the Western Church has decided we can do this thing called living the Christian life without the supernatural power of God. We've concluded that if we study enough and become intellectual enough we can turn the world upside down. But America is dying and going to Hell not for a lack of preaching but for a lack of the supernatural power of the Holy Spirit. There is a generation who are not going to be reached just because we know some things and we entertain them the right way, but they are instead waiting for truth that has the evidence of God's power upon it.

The Baptism of the Holy Spirit is the release of your destiny; it is the release into you of what Jesus died to give you. For you not to believe and receive this is to declare that you are smarter and more pious than Jesus, because Jesus knew He *had* to have the Holy

Spirit to operate in this world.

The Baptist idea today is that "when you are born again, you are baptized into one body" and that is absolutely correct. Yes, you are baptized into Christ and you receive Him completely, but there is another action of the Holy Spirit in your life which is that necessary release.

Signed, Sealed, Delivered

If John 3:16 is the greatest hope for mankind, then Luke 3:16 is the greatest help. Look closely at what Luke recounts of the events of Jesus' baptism:

> "I indeed baptize you with water; but One mightier than I is coming, whose sandal strap I am not worthy to loose. He will baptize you with the Holy Spirit and fire" (Luke 3:16).

Even John knew that there was something beyond the important waters of baptism, and yet Jesus came to John to experience immersion baptism anyway. Read what transpired on that day:

> "When all the people were baptized, it came to pass that Jesus was also baptized; and while He prayed, the heaven was opened. And the Holy Spirit descended in bodily form like a dove upon Him, and a voice came from heaven

which said, 'You are my beloved Son; in You I am well pleased'" (Luke 3:21-22).

Heaven opened up and God pronounced an approval on the person, life, and work of Jesus. The Holy Spirit descended "upon" Him. This is the same word used to describe the action of the Holy Spirit in Acts 2. It was at this moment that Jesus received the "Seal of the Spirit."

It amazes me that so many Christians think they don't need this. Jesus did! He confirmed this later in John's gospel when He said:

"Do not labor for the food which perishes, but for the food which shall endure to everlasting life, which the Son of Man will give you, because God the Father has set His SEAL on Him" (John 6:27).

The opening of Heaven, the administration of that Seal, was a dimensional interruption in the life of Jesus (and it is in ours as well). A portal opened up from Heaven and Jesus was Baptized with the Holy Spirit! God's design is to bring that dimension into our dimension!

In the study of quantum physics we learn that there are eleven dimensions (that we know of so far), and that we live in only four of those. When one of the other seven interrupts ours there is a portal open and the result is that which was impossible becomes a reality! It is called a Miracle!

The Baptism of the Holy Spirit is also a seal of authenticity. In Ephesians 1:13 we read, "In [Jesus] you also trusted, after you heard the word of truth, the gospel of your salvation; in whom also having believed, you were sealed with the Holy Spirit of promise." Here are Paul's words in Ephesians 1:11-13:

> *"In Him also we have obtained an inheri-tance, being predestined according to the purpose of Him who works all things according to the counsel of His will. That we who first trusted in Christ should be to the praise of His glory. In Him you also trusted, after you heard the word of truth, the gospel of your salvation; in whom also having believed, you were sealed with the Holy Spirit of promise."*

The Baptism of the Holy Spirit and the Sealing of the Holy Spirit is the same thing. Being *filled* with the Spirit is different. In Ephesians 5:18-19, Paul wrote:

> *"And do not be drunk with wine, in which is dissipation; but be filled with the Spirit, speaking to one another in psalms and hymns and spiritual songs, singing and making melody in your heart to the Lord."*

So, in one part of the letter Paul discusses an experience he refers to as being "sealed" with the

Holy Spirit, while later he encourages believers to be "filled." It is vital that we understand this distinction. To do so, we have to have a short grammar lesson.

In Ephesians 1:13, the word "sealed" is in what is called the aorist passive tense. The aorist tense conveys an effective, successful, single, one-time-only action. The passive voice indicates that the action was produced by a source outside of the recipient. So, to be "sealed" with the Holy Spirit is a once-and-for-all action that is successfully enacted by God on the life of a believer. If you have been sealed with the Holy Spirit, God did it, not you! He marked you permanently!

However, the word "filled" is in the present imperative tense. This tense conveys a continuous, habitual action that is often reflective of a lifestyle. This is something you do, not just once, but it is something that you endeavor to have happen continually.

A pastor friend of mine tells a story from his younger days when he learned the importance of "being filled."

I was 19 years old when I received the Baptism of the Holy Spirit. Having been raised Baptist, I was aware of the term, and having extended family who were Pentecostal I was casually familiar with the kind of behavior that the event produced. Of course, in my imagination Pentecostals were people who ran around their church in a frenzy, shook violently while blabbering nonsense words, all while holding a rattlesnake in one hand and a cottonmouth in the other. To say I was slightly prejudiced would be a bit of an understatement.

I went to visit my sister's church, and during the altar call I was dragged up onto the podium and I remember the pastor said to me, "Son, your time is right now!" and he laid hands on me, and that was about it for, I was to find out later, about 30 minutes. I was out!

I don't really have any memories of what happened during that time, nor did I receive any special revelation from God that night; outside of the fact that everything I had ever been taught about how He could work in our lives today was completely inaccurate. A couple of weeks later I received the Baptism of the Holy Spirit, and I was completely "wrecked"—if you know what I mean!

A couple of months after that, I was standing in the Sunday night service during the altar call when I felt an urging to go pray for one of my students who was in attendance. I had never done anything like that, but, as the pastor had been preaching on having the faith to go when God tells you to go, I thought it might be a time for me to be tested.

I went into the balcony area where my student was, and I prayed for him. It was the first time I had ever laid hands on anyone. It was the first time that I watched someone I was praying for be slain in the Spirit (and, bear in mind, I was still learning what all of this stuff was).

I have no recollection of how many people I had prayed for when I felt someone tapping on my shoulder. I turned and saw a woman I knew, a member of our church, who had tears in her eyes. She told me that she brought a young woman with her to church that night, and she asked if I would pray for her friend. She directed my attention to a tiny wisp of a woman sitting in a pew near us.

This young lady could not have weighed more than 100 pounds soaking wet. She was seated, but she looked to be perhaps five feet tall. I remember she was wearing a pink and black tracksuit, and she sat there with her arms tightly crossed and slightly rocking back and forth. I eased myself in front of her and asked if I could pray for her. I didn't even wait for a response. I knelt down and laid my hands on her shoulder and head.

I began to pray, or, more accurately, I tried to begin to pray. I couldn't seem to form sentences. I knew what I wanted to say, but it was as if something was distracting the process between my brain and my mouth. I opened my eyes, looked at her face and found myself looking into eyes that were as black as ebony.

That's when I felt the constriction in my

chest. Suddenly, I couldn't breathe. I could inhale, but only in spurts. I tried to stand but my legs were weak. I remember someone helped me stand, and as I moved away another person moved to take my place and that is when all Hell, literally, seemed to break loose.

That little slip of a woman became enraged and lashed out at everyone around her. There was screaming, profanities, hitting, clawing, and kicking at everyone and everything. Even though, the constriction in my chest increased, I was still cognizant enough to watch as she threw off men twice her size that were trying to restrain her.

I began to feel a very real fear. That's when I saw one of the associate pastors walking down the aisle toward the scene as if he were on a pleasant Sunday stroll.

At this point the young woman was on the ground writhing and screaming while being forcibly restrained by two very large men and another man and a cadre of women were praying over her. That's when the associate pastor spoke.

"Gentleman, that's enough," he said calmly. They took their hands off her, and, as they did, she leapt up from the floor and made a move to attack the associate pastor. He was, at least outwardly, completely unfazed. He raised his hand, almost congenially, and said "Demon,

that's enough. You leave that little girl alone."

It was as if she had run into a brick wall. She stumbled backward, and I felt the constriction in my chest ease. She screamed again and ran at the associate pastor. This time, he was not having any of it. He stretched out his arm, pointed at her, and said, "Demon, in Jesus' name, you leave her alone now! Get out of her!"

I watched in amazement as the woman crumpled to the floor. The associate pastor walked over, took her by the hand, and helped her up. He looked her in the face and said, "Sister, it's over if you want it to be."

She seemed to decrease in size before our eyes as she began to cry. I watched as the associate pastor wrapped her up in his arms and embraced her with the love of our Heavenly Father.

A couple of days later, I met with him to talk. I conveyed my amazement at all of this, and, eventually, described my frustration and lack of understanding at what had happened. After all, I had prayed for so many and they seemed to be touched and blessed. What happened with the woman?

"James," he said, "you have to understand, first of all, that God probably did lead you to pray for those people, and, possibly, even that demon-possessed woman. But, I wonder if you

prepared yourself when you felt Him leading you to do so."

"What do you mean?" I asked. I couldn't begin to figure what he meant by that.

"Well, I was there when you received the Baptism of the Holy Spirit. I saw it happen. But, before you began to pray—not just in general, but before each individual—did you ask God to empower you to do the job that He was leading you to do? You are saved, and you have the Holy Spirit living in you, but whenever God leads you to do a work—or, more importantly, whenever He leads you to allow Him to do a work through you—you have to ask that He give you a special endowment of the Holy Spirit to complete that particular work."

We talked for a while after that, but those first sentences are the ones that are with me every day. And I pray that I never again allow myself to be so prideful and dependent on myself that I forget to remember that God is the Source of my strength, and that it is nothing that I do through myself but what I allow Him to do through me. [xviii]

A Wasted Flower

A great actress of the 19th Century stage, Clara Morris, tells a charming story of an unintentional moment of improvisation during her turn as the wronged innocent in the wildly popular play "Camille." She is noted for saying:

> *Somewhere in the world, there is an actor—and a good one—who never eats celery without thinking of me. It was years ago, when I was playing Camille. In the first scene, you will remember, the unfortunate Armand takes a rose from Camille as a token of love. We had almost reached that point, when, as I glanced down, I saw that the flower was missing from its accustomed place on my breast.*
>
> *"What could I do? On the flower hung the strength of the scene. However, I continued my lines in an abstracted fashion, and began a still hunt for that rose or a substitute. My gaze wandered around the stage. On the dinner table was some celery. Moving slowly toward it, I grasped the celery and twisted the tops into a rose form. Then I began the fateful lines:*
>
> *"Take this flower. The life of a camellia is short. If held and caressed it will fade in a morning or an evening."*
>
> *Hardly able to control his laughter, Armand spoke his lines which ran: "It is a cold, scentless flower. It is a wasted flower." I agreed with him.*[xix]

Many brothers and sisters in Christ have done similar twisting to the importance—and even the role

100

—of the Holy Spirit in their lives. Every effort is made to force the Holy Spirit into someone they want Him to be, and His work in their lives into something with which they are comfortable, thereby making the entire experience nothing more than a "wasted flower."

Back in Ephesians 1:13 we are told:

> *"In Him you also trusted, after you heard the word of truth, the gospel of your salvation; in whom also, having believed, you were* **sealed** *with the Holy Spirit of promise."*

Too often, I think, people take this word "seal" and, instead of letting it be done to *them*, they turn it into something they try to do to *the Holy Spirit*.

Please understand that this word "seal" is not meant to convey the sealing of a can. You're not meant to lock the Holy Spirit up inside of you the way you would a sandwich inside a plastic bag. The word, "seal," means a visible brand or mark. It's meant to be seen. The one mark or sign that most people saw in the life of a person who had been baptized in the Holy Spirit was tongues.

So, when does one receive the Holy Spirit? In John 20, Jesus spoke the Great Commission to the disciples. After this, we are told in verse 22 that, "after Jesus said this [the Great Commission] to them, he breathed on them and said to them, 'receive the Holy Ghost'" (John 20:22).

This encounter with the Holy Spirit can best be

understood by looking at the word "breathed." The verse says that the instruction to the disciples was to "receive the sacred (or Holy) breath (or Spirit)." The word "receive" means, simply to "take or receive from another."

Jesus instructed the disciples to receive the Holy Spirit. The first encounter with the Holy Spirit in the life of a believer, then, is a simple act of receiving. Why, then did Jesus not just say "receive the Holy Spirit" and not include the act of breathing on the disciples? The significance of breathing is, conceivably, connected to Genesis 2:7 where God "breathed" into the dust-formed man. This "breath of life" brings about the miracle promised in Ezekiel 36:26: "And I will give you a new heart, and I will put a new spirit within you. And I will take away the stony heart out of your flesh, and I will give you a heart of flesh."

This act of receiving, then, occurs when God breathes new life into the believer at conversion.

Verse 4 of Acts 2 reads: "And tongues as of fire appeared to them, being distributed; and it sat upon each of them." The word translated "sat" does mean "to sit" but there is an implication of sitting for the purposes of taking up residence. As these were tongues of fire, the connection to a supernatural event is clear. The second encounter with the Holy Spirit, then, is that moment where the supernatural power of God is accepted as functioning reality in the life of the believer.

But there is a third type of encounter. The prime

example of this occurs in Acts 4. Peter and John were preaching in the Temple when, "the Sadducees came on them, being grieved that they taught the people, even to announce through Jesus the resurrection from the dead. And they laid hands on them and put them under guard until the next day, for it was already evening." (Acts 4:1-3).

When Peter and John were interrogated, they were asked by whose authority were they preaching, teaching and healing. The Book of Acts recounts that before giving a response, Peter was "filled with the Holy Spirit" (Acts 4:8). This encounter with the Holy Spirit is a fulfillment of the prophecy and promise given by Jesus to the disciples that they should:

> *"Beware of men, for they will deliver you up to the Sanhedrin, and they will scourge you in their synagogues. And you shall be brought before governors and kings for My sake, for a testimony against them and the nations. But when they deliver you up, take no thought how or what you shall speak; for it shall be given you in that same hour what you shall speak. For it is not you who speak, but the Spirit of your Father who speaks in you"* (Matthew 10:17-20).

Why does the Bible recount this as being filled when Peter was already filled with the Holy Spirit on Pentecost? (Acts 2:4). Clearly, in light of Matthew 10 and Acts 4, the believer can expect a third type of

103

encounter with the Holy Spirit. This event is a filling (or a fresh refilling) which prepares the believer for a specific work.

In Acts 8, Luke the Physician recounts the ministry of Philip in Samaria. Upon hearing that many people there had "received the Word of God," the Apostles in Jerusalem sent Peter and John. The Samaritans had not only "received the Word of God," but had also believed, "the things concerning the kingdom of God and the name of Jesus Christ, they were baptized, both men and women" (Acts 8:12).

The Bible states that these Samaritans were believers in Jesus. They were Christians. We're told earlier in Acts 8 that the Samaritan crowds heeded Philip "when they heard and saw all the many miraculous signs which he did" (Acts 8:6).

Many of these same Samaritans were delivered from possession and/or oppression of unclean spirits, and many among them who were paralyzed and lame were healed.

Without question, the manifestations and gifts of the Spirit had already been at work in the lives of the Samaritans through Philip (Acts 8:13). The interesting part of the narrative, for our purposes here, begins in verse 15 of chapter 8. Again, the account states that the apostles in Jerusalem heard what was happening in Samaria and, so, sent Peter and John to them. We are told that Peter and John prayed for the Samaritans," that they might receive the Holy Ghost" (Acts 8:15).

It is interesting to note that all of the "require-ments" (i.e., a confession of faith in Jesus Christ followed by baptism) had already been met by the Samaritans for whom Peter and John were praying that they might receive the Holy Ghost.

Then in verse 16 we are told that Peter and John prayed this for the Samaritans specifically because "for as yet [the Holy Spirit] was fallen upon none of them: only they were baptized in the name of the Lord Jesus" (Acts 8:16).

Clearly, the Samaritans were Christians. They heard the gospel from Philip, believed, and were baptized. They received physical healing and saw other "mighty works" (Acts 8:13). But it was not until Peter and John came to minister and prayed for a special encounter with the Holy Spirit, specifically because they had not had the Spirit fall on them, that they received the Holy Spirit.

This is ample evidence to support the existence, and ergo, the doctrinal viability, of a "second blessing" of *something*. While it may not be tongues necessarily, it is another distinguishable act of blessing by God in the life of the believer that occurs after the point of salvation.

CHAPTER 8

THE WIND BLOWS WHERE IT WILL

*A church in the land without the Spirit is
rather a curse than a blessing. If you have not
the Spirit of God, Christian worker, remember
that you stand in somebody else's way;
you are a fruitless tree standing where
a fruitful tree might grow.* [xx]

– CHARLES SPURGEON

It is a common plot in American television. The lonely depressed ex-husband, left by his wife years prior and still lonely. During the Christmas season he brings out the old, still wrapped presents. Most are for her, but maybe one is for him. The television show *Monk*, used this to great effectiveness. For the most part, the show was written where a new crime was solved every week. But the umbrella of the story was the one crime that Monk couldn't solve: the murder of his wife.

She was killed in a car-bombing—and Monk was

certain the bomb was intended for him. Every year, he brought out his Christmas decorations and placed the one gift that he still had from his wife, Trudy, under the tree. Friends tried to convince him that he should open it, that they were sure Trudy would want him to have it. Still, Monk refused. To open it would be to throw away the last thing that was still her.

Unfortunately (and this is a small spoiler in case you have not seen the show) the contents of the gift proved to be the key that opened the door to solving her murder. The key was there in his own apartment for over twelve agonizing years, but he refused to open the gift.

This chapter is a difficult one to write because I believe that most of the American Church has this same problem. We live in frustration, confusion, and despair; we long for clarity and purpose; we desperately cry out to God for answers, all the while He is looking down on us and saying, "I've already given it to you! Why don't you receive the gift! Open the box!"

Lingo Language

In today's American Church, we love our catch phrases. We are completely enamored with our Christian lingo, buzzwords, and church-ese. Learning these words is part of the process of "getting in" and the ability to spot people who aren't quite there with us hinges on being able to tell if they know these words and phrases or not. Even knowing them sometimes is not enough.

I have a friend who is a professor at a Christian University. He tells the story of the first class of the semester where he was making introductions. He casually asked, "Can I assume that all of us are 'Christians,' whatever that word might mean to you?"

For him, it was a normal part of the start-of-term process that he used to get into a different part of the opening lecture, but He was surprised when one young woman raised her hand. When he acknowledged her, she said, "Professor, I don't really consider myself a Christian. I'm a Christ-follower."

This is not the time or place to talk about how this one line of demarcation is infiltrating the church, but it's interesting to see how it has become so normative.

There are other words, though, that few would question. However, that is exactly what I intend to do here. This flies in the face of a firmly entrenched idea in the history of Christianity, but understanding this can be a step toward complete emancipation in the life of the believer. Let's go back to the rooftop conversation Jesus had with Nicodemus.

You Must Be... What Now?

We've already touched, very briefly, on the well-known conversation that Jesus had with the Pharisee

Nicodemus. However, to understand how intrinsically connected salvation is with the experience of Holy Spirit baptism, we must see how Jesus taught them as inextricably intertwined. Let's look again at the conversation found in John 3:

> *"Jesus answered and said unto him, 'Most assuredly I say to you, unless one is born again, he cannot see the kingdom of God.' Nicodemus said to Him, 'How can a man be born when he is old? Can he enter a second time into his mother's womb and be born'?*
>
> *Jesus answered, 'Most assuredly, I say to you, unless one is born of water and the Spirit, he cannot enter the kingdom of God. That which is born of the flesh is flesh, and that which is born of the Spirit is Spirit. Do not marvel that I say to you, you must be born again. The wind blows where it wishes, and you hear the sound of it, but cannot tell where it comes from and where it goes. So is everyone who is born of the Spirit'"* (John 3:3-8).

Before we can proceed, I have to prepare you for the fact that I am about to write what is sure to be one of the most unpopular sentences a preacher could ever pen. The term "born again" is wrong.

I know that plants an enormous load of TNT right beneath one of the Church's favorite, and most ingrained, buzzwords, but it is, quite simply, not correct. This phrase in Greek is *gennao anothen*. And, to be fair there is nothing "wrong" with the translation, "born again," but it simply does not convey the full force of meaning inherent in the Greek text.

Gennao is from another word which means "to procreate," and implies not only birth but to be regenerated by the work of another. The word *anothen* is best translated "from above." Consequently, the phrase that has become a cornerstone of our understanding of the salvation experience is better translated: "Unless one is born of another from above."

Jesus tells Nicodemus that unless a person is born of another from above, he cannot see the Kingdom of God.

So, is this really connected to the idea of the Baptism of the Holy Spirit? Absolutely! Look at what Jesus says are the two requirements: being born of water *and* Spirit. Without meeting these requirements, a person cannot enter the Kingdom of God.

Jesus, then goes on to use what sounds like poetic language to make His point. "The wind blows where it wishes, and you hear the sound of it, but cannot tell where it comes from and where it goes. So is everyone who is born of the Spirit" (John 3:8).

This word "Spirit" is tricky. In verse 6, it has a literal meaning of "wind or breath" while figuratively meaning "spirit" or, more specifically, "God's Spirit."

In classical theology, we get our word *pneuma-tology,* or the study of things related to the Holy Spirit, from this word. However, in verse 8, the word for wind is very similar to that used in verse 6. Early Church Fathers: Tertullian, Chrysostom, and others interpreted these words—*Spirit* in verse 6, and *wind* in verse 8—as the same word!

Additionally, the word used in verse 8 that is translated as "hear" is noteworthy. Normally in the Greek text, "hear" is almost always the Greek word *acuo*—we get "acoustic" from this—but in this verse it is the word *phone.* It doesn't simply mean "to hear" but it refers to hearing caused by the act of speech or spoken language. So, verse 8 can be read as follows: "The Spirit Spirits where He wills and you HEAR the SOUND of HIM."

Jesus is saying, "Nicodemus, the Spirit is like a wind in control of a man. And when He is in control you will hear that man articulate a language or sound that comes from the Spirit. So is EVERYONE who is born of the Spirit!"

There you have it! The Baptism of the Spirit is the mark to release through you the fullness of Christ and His Kingdom!

A Word of Caution

If you begin to cry out ABBA Father and get alone with God, I assure you He will speak through you! But you have to *say* it! Seek after tongues, and don't ever forbid the use of them. But don't seek the gift without using a thousand times more energy seeking the Giver.

Seek God! Why? Because the natural man can receive nothing of the Spirit. "I was raised to believe…," you might say, but it doesn't matter if what you were raised to believe was wrong.

It's both funny and sad to me that Western Civilization, specifically Western Europe and America, are the only group in the whole world who have tried to dismiss the supernatural. We're the only part of the greater Church that has excused the Holy Spirit from our lives. We just don't need Him!

Paul had a similar problem to deal with from members of the Corinthian church. In his first letter to them, the apostle wrote these words, reminding them of an early warning and prophecy from Isaiah:

"…with men of other tongues and other lips I will speak to this people; And yet for all that they will not hear me" (1 Corinthians 14:21).

There are individuals who insist that this phrase "other tongues" and that this passage in general have nothing to do with tongues, but is, instead, about judgment. Well, it is certainly about judgment, yet it's talking about both. To approach the understanding of this passage systematically, you have to go back to Isaiah and see what the full context was. Read the original passage:

"...whom will he make to understand the message? Those just weaned from milk? Those just drawn from the breasts? For precept must be upon precept, precept upon precept, line upon line, here a little there a little. For with stammering lips and another tongue he will speak to this people to whom he said this is the rest with which you may cause the weary to rest. And this is the refreshing yet they would not hear. But the word of the Lord was to them, Precept upon precept, precept upon precept, line upon line, line upon line, here a little, there a little, they might go and fall backward and be broken and snared and caught" (Isaiah 28:9-13).

Isaiah makes use of sarcasm in this text. Look at the opening questions. "You're acting like babies and yet you want to try to understand this message?" He intimates that these are people who nitpick every little thing and question it to death (line upon line, precept upon precept. They hear it like this: "I know preacher, but what about...? Yeah, ok, but what about...?" Instead of receiving what is being said), so that every aspect of the message loses its power. They refuse to receive revelation, because they are so caught up in the law.

The prophet goes on to say that God informs them that He, God, is going to rock their world by making a new revelation using people with stammering lips and other tongues. Doing this will give rest to the weary. If you embrace tongues, you are able to do things that you can't do on your own ("For we know not how to pray as we should…") and it gives rest.

Finally, the Lord says that even though He gives this gift, this rest, this refreshing, people would still refuse to accept it. Why? Because they couldn't get a revelation from the Lord beyond, "Precept upon precept, precept upon precept, line upon line, line upon line, here a little, there a little" and what would the result be? They would "fall backward and be broken and snared and caught."

This is exactly what happened to the Pharisees in Jesus' day. They had grown so accustomed to believing that they had all the answers, because they had studied so hard and embraced their traditional teachings, that they forced God into a box. When Jesus came along, He didn't look like what they expected, so they dismissed Him out of hand. They were so busy trying to figure God out that they missed all of the places in their own scriptures where they were told to "faith" God out.

In America today, we still do this. We say to God, "Give us just enough of the Spirit to see people saved and make us feel good, but don't go too far!" And this is why the Church in America and Western Europe is frustrated. We try to serve by our intellect, by our theology, by our systems and our doctrines, but we have lost the ability to serve God with faith—and it has caused us to be caught in a snare of our own making!

The Baptism of the Holy Spirit is the seal of God on your life! In the ancient world, a seal was a mark of approval, authenticity, authority, and ability. The seal opened the doors to places others could not go. It also kept you out of places you didn't *need* to enter. The seal brought you favor. Why would you not want to be marked by God?

If you are sealed or marked there is a *sound* or expression in you! You can speak in tongues! It is in you! It is a precious gift!

CHAPTER 9

TAKE WHAT'S YOURS

Every time I took a long leave from home,
I felt as if I were going to conquer the world.
Or rather, take possession of what is
my birthright, my inheritance. [xxi]

– ELLA MAILLART

I love the parables of Jesus. I really do. But I can't say I care for the Parable of the Prodigal Son. Or, more to the point, I don't like the title.

Of course, Jesus is hardly to blame for the title. He never sat down and said, "Let me tell you the story of 'The Prodigal Son.'" Then what is my problem with this particular parable?

It's all about focus. Look at how the story begins. In Luke 15:11 it reads, "Then [Jesus] said: 'A certain man had two sons.'"

Now, it may seem like I'm being nitpicky, but Jesus didn't start the parable by saying, "There were once two sons." He began, "A certain *man...*" This is not a story about a prodigal son. It isn't even one about a prodigal son and a thrifty son. This is a story about The Faithful Father. We are all familiar with the account.

The prodigal son asks for his half of the father's wealth, and the father gives it to him. The prodigal then proceeds to go out and live life recklessly and promiscuously until all of the money is squandered. He has nothing left, and, rather than return to his father, he finds himself living with pigs.

Finally, one day, the Bible records, the prodigal son "came to himself" and remembered that the servants in his father's house were living exponentially better than he was. The young man contrived a grand and glorious speech of contrition and set off for home.

But look at the phrase in Luke 15:20. The Bible says that "when [the prodigal son] was *still a great way off*, his father saw him and had compassion and *ran* and fell on his neck and kissed him" (emphases mine).

The father saw that wayward boy, not when he knocked on the door of the house, not when someone informed the father that his lost son had returned. The son wasn't even close to town. When the boy was "still a *great* way off" the father saw him because he had been actively looking for him to return.

Excited, the father interrupts the boy's contrition speech and tells a servant to take care of the young man's tattered, smelly clothes, put a clean and beautiful robe on him, give him a ring (a mark of authority), and sandals—and to kill the fatted calf. It was party time!

Then there's the other brother. He faithfully stayed at home and worked hard for his father. But he never enjoyed the fruits of his labor nor the benefits of living in his father's house. He felt the need to labor for his dad's approval. Look at what happened when he returned from a hard day in the fields. A servant greeted him, saying, "Your brother has come, and because he has received him safe and sound, your father has killed the fatted calf."

And what was this other brother's response? Luke 15:28 says, "he was angry and would not go in."

Imagine that! All this time, his only brother was, for all intents and purposes, dead, and his response to hearing that his brother is alive and well was to get angry. So upset in fact that he refused to even attend the party and acknowledge his sibling's existence.

His father came out and pleaded with him. But this young man responded by making what I am sure was, to his way of thinking, a sound and reasonable argument. He explained, "I've been working for you all this time. It's been years that I've served you. I never broke a single rule of your house. I did everything you asked, and you never even gave me a goat to kill so that I could have a nice informal dinner with my friends. But this loser shows up after being gone all this time, after wasting half of your entire fortune on loose women and partying, and for him you kill the fatted calf we've been saving for a special occasion!"

Now for the final proof that this story is really the

Parable of The Faithful Father. The father replied, "Son, you are always with me, and *all that I have is yours.*" This poor boy didn't understand that he wasn't living according to what was already his. He was, instead, living his entire life:

- To get approval that he already had.
- To obtain an inheritance that was already his.
- To receive gifts that his father wanted to lavish on him.

My Father's World

I love my children. They are mine by birth and by blood. They enjoy everything I have and carry everything I am. They had no choice in the matter. All that I am became theirs by birth and blood. Nothing they ever do will make them more my children than they already are. My DNA is in them. They are mine, and I am theirs.

Our Heavenly Father is like that. He owns the cattle on a thousand hills, the hills, what grows on the hills, what lives in the hills, and all of the minerals under the hills. It's all His!

The good news is this: God loves you not because of who you are, but because of who He is, because that is His character. He blesses you not because of who you are, but because of who He is since that's His nature.

Your Heavenly Father has already given to you

eternally everything you were ever going to have because it's all part of the "package deal" that Jesus created at Calvary and through the resurrection.

The world of religion has driven into us the concept that we have to work for God's approval. Even those who come from a culturally religious background that is primarily Calvinistic (the champions of grace) tend to train their adherents to operate in the performance trap. All of this to obtain God's favor and approval.

This is your Father's world! Why would you ever want to live like the "frugal brother" and work your life away trying to achieve something you already possess? You have a choice to make. Will you strive for something that God has already given and live in bondage to legalism, or will you walk out your inheritance by faith?

That Man Job Had Nothing On Me

The book of Job is, by all scholarly accounts, the oldest book in the Bible. I think that might be important. It is significant, in my mind, that the oldest book in Scripture contains the account of bad things— *really* bad things—happening to, by God's own description, a "good man."

It gives me hope and comfort knowing that when unfortunate things take place in my life, I have biblical proof that God knows about them, is looking out for me, and that Satan, in all that time, has learned approximately zero new tricks. It also comforts me that

Job did his very best to endure with patience the trial that had come upon him. I also take solace in the fact that, even though Job had done nothing wrong, his friends' only real help was to cast aspersions on his character and say that he somehow must have brought it all on himself

Ultimately, I find comfort that when he just couldn't take it anymore, Job finally questioned God, and the Almighty didn't strike him down for being impertinent.

Sometimes I find myself wondering why I'm going through a certain trial or test; why has God allowed these terrible things to happen to me, to my family, to our church? Then I read Job and am reminded that God is patient and loves me through all of my questions. Sometimes, He even answers them.

In Job 31:2, that poor, pitiful man had reached his breaking point. He asks, "For what is the allotment of God from above, and the inheritance of the Almighty from on high?" Essentially, Job said "I want to know who You are, what You have for me, and how I obtain it." That's not a bad thing to ask. Do you want everything that God has for you?

Again, the good news is, you can't work for your Heavenly Father's favor, and you will never be holy enough to earn it. In Christ, at this very moment, you are as eternally holy as you will ever be. Most people don't believe that because of their flesh.

It is the flesh that refuses to receive what God has for you, but your flesh is not who you are. You are who your spirit is. And God declared that you are holy and righteous—and already in possession of a marvelous inheritance.

In Ephesians 1:11, we read these amazing words:

> *"In [Jesus] also we have obtained an INHER-ITANCE, being predestined according to the purpose of Him who works all things according to the council of His will. That we who first trusted in Christ should be to the praise of His glory. In whom you also trusted, after you heard the word of truth, the gospel of your salvation; in whom also having believed you were SEALED with the Holy Spirit of Promise! Who is the guarantee of our INHERITANCE until the redemption of the purchase possession, to the praise of His glory."*

Inheritance, Inheritance, INHERITANCE! You already have it!

We've mentioned the importance of understanding the Baptism of the Holy Spirit as the Seal, but it is just as vital to understand the Baptism of the Holy Spirit as the "guarantee" of our inheritance. What does this mean?

Nothing Down

If you've ever purchased a house, you know the process. If you haven't, you may not know the intricacies of home-buying, but it's very helpful, both practically and theologically, to know the steps.

It's time to buy a house, so you decide to start looking. First you shore up your credit and aim for a home you can really afford. You talk to your lender and get approved for a certain price range. Now comes the fun part. You consider home size, number of bedrooms, location, school systems and square footage. You decide between ranch style or round-house, A-Frame or I-house, Cottage or Chalet, American Colonial or Cape Dutch, Bungalow or Barndominium, Federal or Faux Chateau, Gambrel or Gablefront, Manor or Manufactured House, Saltbox or Split-Level, Microhouse or McMansion. Then you find homes in your area that meet your criteria.

You go on what seems like an endless parade of uncomfortable tours of people's homes (unless the home is empty), and finally find one that is absolutely perfect. It is everything you could ever want. You make an offer. They say no, but make a counteroffer of slightly more money. It's still within your range (and what you were willing to pay anyway, because, let's face it, nobody opens with a reasonable bid), so you accept. Now the realtor asks the question:

And how much will you be paying in earnest money?

People tend to think that earnest money is a down payment. It isn't. The down payment is what a person pays at closing. It's all the money your lender didn't give you. The earnest payment is what you pay to the seller to demonstrate your sincerity in the offer you have made to make the purchase. Sometimes, this money is returned to and folded into the purchase price, and, in some cases, it is simply a good faith payment to the seller. It is a small taste of the greater amount of money yet to come.

This earnest money or "earnest payment" has been called various things throughout the years. Whether known as a "good-faith payment," an "earnest penny" or an "Arles penny," the oldest known term for this payment was *Argentum Dei* or "God's Penny." It signified money given to bind a bargain. No deal was ever considered serious until earnest money was paid.

Now, think about how God led Paul to speak about the gift of the Holy Spirit to us. He said, "[The Holy Spirit] is the *guarantee* of our inheritance until the redemption of the purchase possession."

God has given us an earnest payment of our inheritance. He has said, "I want you to know that I am serious about this deal I'm making with you. I'm promising to give you an inheritance of ME, that you will sit with ME in Heavenly places, that you will have grace, mercy, love, and direction from ME, that I will never leave you nor forsake you. And just so you know how serious I am, I am going to take 'the same spirit that raised Jesus from the dead' (Romans 8:11) and put Him in you so that in your living death, you will be more alive than you can imagine. You will get a taste of the wonders of Heaven during the hardship of living in a fallen world."

That gift of the Holy Spirit—the baptism that empowers us to live as God wants us to live, that enables us to do the things that the Lord has prepared us to do, that gets us ready for the obstacles the enemy wants to throw our way, that puts the right words in our mouths at just the right time—should never be thought of, much less treated, like a wasted flower. It is the promise of our inheritance. We should embrace it!

Right Your Tongues

Before leaving this subject, it must be pointed out that, yes tongues is significant. However, far too many Christians believe that when they were baptized in the Holy Spirit and spoke in tongues that they got everything God had for them. We have to think about it like this: Your Abba is teaching you how to talk (among many other things), but have you grown up?

It was cute when my little babies started blabbering "dadadadada" or "mamamama," but, by the time they're four or five, there was an expectation that they know my name, so that, if we were out and about and were accidentally separated then they would be able to tell a person to whom they belonged. Even more so, when they are full-grown adults, they should be able to articulate more.

In Corinth, Paul had to deal with the problem of

the believers getting hung up on baby talk and acting like toddlers. In his first letter, Paul spends a good deal of time breaking down spiritual gifts, what they are, and what their purpose is. Paul then, in reference to these chapters and then his note in chapter 13 regarding the need for maturity, offers a very strange rebuke in chapter 14:

> *"Brethren, do not be children in understanding; however, in malice be babes, but in understanding be mature"* (1 Corinthians 14:20).

How odd it is that Paul would say to these Spirit-filled Christians that their behavior was child-like, and this was couched in his teaching about spiritual gifts. The short answer had already been stated: as you grow, not simply in chronological age but in maturity, your understanding should grow as well.

Consider again what Paul said to the Corinthian believers. Tongues are not, ultimately, a gift solely for the speaker. They are, instead:

> *"...a sign, not to those who believe but to unbelievers; but prophesying is not for unbelievers but for those who believe. Therefore if the whole church comes together in one place, and all speak with tongues, and there come in those who are uninformed or unbelievers, will they not say that you are out of your mind? But*

if all prophesy, and an unbeliever or an unin-formed person comes in, he is convinced by all, he is convicted by all. And thus the secrets of his heart are revealed; and so, falling down on his face, he will worship God and report that God is truly among you" (1Corinthians 14:22-25).

Tongues exist, in part, to function as a gift that reveals the secrets of the unbeliever's heart. This revelation will cause him to fall on his face and worship God.

This is not to say that tongues does not benefit the believer individually. In Romans 8, Paul writes:

"...likewise the Spirit also helps in our weaknesses. For when we do not know what we should pray for as we ought, but the Spirit Himself makes intercession for us with groaning which cannot be uttered" (Romans 8:26).

Do you ever have that feeling that you just can't put into words what is going on in your heart, your spirit, your mind? That's when the Spirit makes intercession. A young pastor I know once had an encounter with God that he describes as:

"It was the most intense experience I've ever known. I was at my most frustrated. I knew I was called into ministry, but absolutely no

doors were opening. The sky seemed to have turned to brass. I felt totally alone.

I grabbed my Bible, went into my bedroom, fell on my knees, and prayed the most honest prayer I had ever uttered in my life. It sounded something like, "GAAAAHHHHD!" followed by a half hour of sobbing. In between my sobs I tried to articulate what was in my head, but it just came out in sounds such as I had never imagined..."

The work of the Holy Spirit should not, and must not, be distilled down to simply speaking in tongues. However, it is part of the outward sign of the mark, the seal, that God places on and in the life of the believer. It is a mark of inheritance, an earnest payment, *God's Penny* to you which demonstrates His sincerity in providing for you an inheritance full of riches so great that you could barely imagine.

CHAPTER 10

INHERITANCE

I wish you to observe how real and beneficial the religion of Christ is to a man about to die... This is all the inheritance given to my dear family. The religion of Christ which will give them one which will make them rich indeed. [xxii]

— PATRICK HENRY

In closing this effort to unveil the secrets contained in The Mystery of the One New Man, it is beneficial and important to take a moment to talk about the specific portion of your inheritance as a grafted-in child of God, living in the fulfillment of the creation of the One New Man.

The Allocation of Your Inheritance

In the details of a last will and testament, a person usually divides their estate not simply among people, but as an apportioned parceling to a single individual. God is no different. So in the entirety of this inheritance, how has God distributed that blessing to you?

131

His Abiding Presence

In Psalm 16:5, we read, "O Lord, You are the portion of my inheritance and my cup. You maintain my lot."

The psalmist declares that God is your fulfillment and your future. It's like the old saying, "I don't know what the future holds, but I know Who holds the future." That's true, except it doesn't go far enough. According to this psalm, God Himself is your future.

His Abundant Provision

As the One New Man, you do not have to strive for what is yours. The psalmist writes, "...the lines have fallen to me in pleasant places. Yes, I have a good inheritance" (Psalm 16:6).

God makes provision for you. And because He does, you don't just have a meager inheritance, not one that will tide you over until something better comes along, but instead you have a *good* inheritance.

His Supernatural Instruction

In Psalm 16:7, we discover that God has crafted a way to educate us that goes beyond the natural. The psalmist says, "I will bless the Lord who has given me counsel; My heart also instructs me in the night seasons."

THE MYSTERY OF THE ONE NEW MAN

God gives dreams and visions as a means to guide us into and through the Mystery of the One New Man.

His Immovable Faith

We discussed early in this book a startling truth: that we do not live by our own faith, or even the faith that is given to us by God, but we live instead by the faith of Jesus Christ Himself. In Psalm 16:8, we read, "I have set the Lord always before me; because He is at my right hand I shall not be moved."

In Jesus Christ we have—not *can* have, but *have*—authority, confidence and steadfastness. We don't ever have to go backwards, but, as my friend Ken Hartley wrote in his song, "Press On," we can:

> *Forget what is behind and press on to what's ahead.*
> *What is done is done, what's been said has been said.*
> *With my past under the blood and by His Spirit led,*
> *I forget what is behind and press on to what's ahead.* [xxiii]

His Assurance and Peace

The One New Man has absolutely no need to fear, be anxious, or riddled with worry. This is because God

Himself is your peace! Since this is true, we can agree with the psalmist and delight, "Therefore my heart is glad, and my glory rejoices. My flesh also will rest in hope" (Psalm 16:9).

His Deliverance

Do you ever feel like you're just withering away? That there is nothing real or meaningful for you in this world? If you are in Christ, this feeling does not come from embracing your inheritance in the One New Man. The psalmist declares in 16:10, "...for you [God] will not leave my soul in Sheol."

You have been delivered, body, mind, and soul, from your past. All you have to do now is live the deliverance of your inheritance.

His Holiness And Preservation

The psalmist continues that thought by taking it a step further. He says not only will you not leave my soul in Sheol, but "nor will you allow your Holy One to see corruption." You are, as the One New Man, already holy and resurrected. Satan cannot touch you! He has no power over you at all. Why? Because God has promised to make you holy and preserve you!

His Direction

Do you ever wonder which path you should take?

Should you accept that new job or stay where you are? Move to a new city or remain where you feel you are called? God provides direction for us, as the psalmist says in 16:11, "You [God] will show me the path of life." Not only will God direct you, but He will lead you into a vibrant, meaningful future.

His Contentment and Joy

Placement is important, but it is not about geography. Rather, it is completely about proximity to the Father. In Psalm 16:11 we read, "...in Your presence is fullness of joy." This is not a joy that is partial or incomplete. When you allow yourself to bathe in the closeness and immediacy of God's presence, that is where and when you experience joy fully and completely.

His Eternal Pleasures

The psalmist closes out the explanation of the benefits found in God's presence by saying in 16:11, "...at Your right hand are pleasures forevermore." Understand that this is not "pleasures" in the sense of the indulgence and vice that Pinocchio and Lampwick found on Pleasure Island. Moreover, these pleasures are not transient. They last, according to the psalmist, "forever more."

The Assurance of Your Inheritance

So often we hear about squandered inheritances. Trustee babies such as the Kardashians and the Hiltons dominate the news. There are even stories of parents pilfering the trusts left to their children by grandparents. It's all too easy to think of your God-given inheritance in earthly terms, but don't entertain that kind of thinking. You can have certain assurances from God about your inheritance. In Psalm 37, we read about these assurances and how we can rest in them today!

Riches That Remain

Far too frequently, we have heard stories of everyday people who hit a lottery worth millions upon millions of dollars only to be destitute a few years later. The psalmist tells us that, in our inheritance, we have more than we ever need, and, not only that, but it is better than the wealth accumulated by the unjust. He says, "A little that a righteous man has is better than the many riches of the wicked" (Psalm 37:16).

We know that our inheritance is not a small matter, so, if the little we have is so much greater than the riches accumulated by the wicked, how much more is the whole of our inheritance from God?

Purpose That Prevails

Much has been spoken and written of in the past

several years regarding purpose. Whatever God has for you to do is your calling, but your purpose is to worship God and declare His glory.

Can you have assurance that this purpose will be sustained? Psalm 37:17 reminds us, "For the arms of the wicked shall be broken but the Lord upholds the upright." Yes, your purpose will prevail!

Unfailing Faithfulness

Psalm 37:18 tells us, "The Lord knows the days of the upright." How wonderful it is that the Lord Himself knows the end from the beginning. He watches over us. His faithfulness is, as the well-known hymn says, truly great!

Yes, you have a number on your life. There are some who believe that God has given us 70 years, others say 120 years, but you cannot prove from the Hebrew that this is what God has ordered. Instead, the Bible tells us our days are numbered.

The Hebrew language doesn't give permission to conclude that if someone dies before they turn seventy, then it's because they had some unrepentant sin. What it does say is that you have a number, and when you are walking in the divine providence and supernatural protection of God—in short, when you choose to walk in your inheritance—then nothing can change God's plans. But, by the same token, you can live in willful sin and shorten your life.

Infinite Inheritance

Again, we have mentioned the trust that so many place in earthly wealth, but money has a way of slipping through our fingers. A godly inheritance, however, freely flows from His throne of grace. Psalm 37:18 concludes by saying that, just as God knows the days of the upright, "their inheritance shall be forever." I'm going to talk about this word "forever" again in just a moment.

Confidence That Conquers

So does living out the mystery of the One New Man, and embracing your inheritance mean that hard times will never find us? Sadly, no. However, in Psalm 37:19, we read that, for those who have chosen to claim their inheritance, "they shall not be ashamed in the evil time." What does that really mean? In the Hebrew, it translates that "in the days of wickedness they shall not hang their heads in disappointment."

So, yes, there will be difficult times. Jesus Himself said that we would have trouble in the world, but that we should not be afraid because He has overcome the world. If you know who you are and what you have, then you can live in total confidence.

Abundance That Abounds In Adversity

Psalm 37:19 gives this promise to those who

embrace their inheritance: "...in the days of famine they shall be satisfied." Even though hard times may surface, when they arrive, you can still be satisfied.

This requires a level of self-discipline. Too often I see people who want the rewards of a lifetime of hard work when they are just starting out. A twenty-year-old fresh out of college is probably not going to earn what someone who has been working for five decades will, nor should he. He won't have the trappings of that life—the house or the car or the amenities—and that's okay. Because those lean years are a time for you to grow and strengthen the muscles of your self-discipline and create a soil in your heart that is prepared for the seed that God wants to plant in you.

It's been said time and again, but it's still true, that if God can't trust you with a little, there's no way you will be entrusted with a lot.

When He sees your faith, belief, and trust, you will walk in an abundance that baffles those around you. Observers may question, "You lost your job because of unfair cutbacks and salary raises for people who could buy and sell you? I'm so sorry! How can you still be making it? I see cars in your driveway, there's food on your table, and your bills are being paid. How is this possible?"

That's when you are able brag on your Daddy and talk about the abundance that rests in your inheritance.

Enemies Are Eliminated

If you spend two minutes, ten hours, ten days, ten months, or ten years stressing over one enemy, something is wrong. Jesus put your adversary in his place by speaking one word to him, and it was over.

Too often Christians forget that the only real enemy they have is Satan, and he's already been defeated. So, if he's vanquished, you can use the same weapon Jesus used against him: the Word.

The Word of God is sharper than any two-edged sword. Go ahead and use it! Please note that much of the time, what we wrestle with is not the devil, but is, instead, our flesh. Use the same sword to cut that dead weight off of you, and boldly walk in your victory.

What do we do when foes rise up against us? We are given every reason not to worry when we read in Psalm 37:20, "...the wicked shall perish and the enemies of the Lord like the splendor of the meadows shall vanish into smoke they shall vanish away."

Debts Are Dissolved

In Psalm 37:21 we have this statement which includes an inferred promise. The psalmist writes, "...the wicked borrows and does not repay but the righteous shows mercy and gives."

Is it wrong to borrow money for anything and not

repay it? Yes! But what else does this verse say? It tells us that the righteous show mercy and are giving in their wealth, but inherent in that is the idea that if a person is righteous, then God will see to it that this state—being able to show mercy and to give freely—will be conferred on that person. God will work with you to dissolve your debt.

Riches Are Redirected

How does God accomplish this? In Psalm 37:22 we're told that "those blessed by Him shall inherit the earth. But those cursed by Him shall be cut off." The Lord will separate blessing from those who are wicked, and He will give, instead, to His children the inheritance of the earth. Why? Because...

The Four D's

God makes this happen because your Daddy is Delighted to Direct your Destiny.

Psalm 37:23 tells us that that "the steps of a good man are ordered by the Lord and He delights in his way."

Too often this verse has been interpreted to mean that the "he" is treated as a reference to the "good man." It isn't. This statement says that God orders the good man's steps because He, God, is delighted by the good man's ways."

Additionally, the language in the verse does not picture the Lord picking your feet up and placing them somewhere, but instead shows Him walking before us, leading the way He wants us to go, and then we follow—stretching our legs and feet to keep in perfect step with the Father.

Success Is Secured

What this means, then, is that even though we mess up in our efforts to walk in Daddy's footprints, He is there to ensure our eventual success. Psalm 37:24 declares, "Though [you] fall [you] shall not be utterly cast down. For the Lord upholds [you] with His hand."

God is not sitting back in Heaven waiting to lay a supernatural smackdown on you when you make mistakes. He is leading your way, and is there to lift you when you fall.

Legacy Is Lasting

Read Psalm 37:25-26. It begins by saying, "I have been young, and now am old…" At first glance, this is depressing until you understand the context. The psalmist (here it's King David), says once I was young and made stupid mistakes. There were Bathsheba moments, and I failed both as a father and as a follower; I failed as a king and as a servant, but in all of that, "I have not seen the righteous forsaken nor his descendants begging bread."

David confessed how he broke the faith time and again with his family, his subjects, and his men, but God "is ever merciful and lends." Even when it seemed all hope was lost, he found that with the Almighty, "His descendants are blessed."

If you are walking in the promise of your inheritance as the One New Man, even your children will receive a portion of that inheritance.

To summarize the understanding of the allocation and assurance of your inheritance, let me invite you to pray this prayer with me:

Abba, as You continue to reveal the mysteries of the One New Man, help me every day to understand that I can enjoy the privilege of Your presence and provision, that You have promised to give me guidance and instruction which eclipses that of human understanding, that You have given me resolute faith, assurance and peace.

You have delivered me into Your holiness and preservation. You show me the path my life is to take and You allow me to linger in Your presence where there is contentment, joy, and pleasures forever more.

Help me to remember that, in You, I have true riches and purpose, because You are faithful in Your promises. In You, I can be confident that my inheritance has within it an abundance that I can't imagine, that in You I am secure from Your enemies, that You will turn their wealth over to me not so I can live lavishly, but so I can lavishly love others in Your name.

Thank You, Lord, that You delight to lead me in my destiny, and that, because of You, my success is secure and my legacy is lasting. I praise You, Lord, that I am the One New Man called according to Your purpose, for Your glory and the advancement of Your Kingdom.

In Jesus' name. Amen.

CHAPTER 11

ACTIVATING YOUR
INHERITANCE

The devil will let a preacher
prepare a sermon if it will keep him
from preparing himself. [xxiv]
— VANCE HAVNER

Think back for a moment to the people we have discussed in this book: Whitney Cerak and Laura Van Ryn, songwriter Bill Gaither, actor and director Mel Gibson, actor Jim Caviezel, Sarah Dunn Clarke, homeless millionaire Tomas Martinez, Paula Abdul, Hugh Laurie, Charlie Sheen, Simon Cowell, Robert Downey Jr., Adam Sandler, Brad Pitt, Johnny Depp, Will Smith, Mark Zuckerberg, billionaire Larry Ellison, Andy Griffith and Don Knotts, Russell Brand, Britney Spears, Michael Sattler, Ron Phillips, and Clara Morris. Not an unimpressive list of names. Some of these are known far and wide, while others barely register a blip on the radar of public awareness. But I want you to add a name to this list: your own.

You see, from God's perspective, there is no difference in design, desire, or destiny for any person we have mentioned. He designed you! He knows you intimately!

God not only knows everything about you, but He also knew it before you did. He longs to engage in relationship with you. He desires you! Why? Because before the first breath of "Let there be…" was ever uttered, the Creator knew all there was to know about you and had pre-destinied your life to be conformed to His will and purpose.

But the Lord forces nothing on any individual. I have heard people say that Hell is the ultimate power trip, because God says "Do it my way or else" and then when He gives you the free will to make your own decisions, you wind up in Hell for them.

My friend, God sends no one to Hell. If you end up in there, then you do so, along with every other person who has been too prideful to return the embrace of their Heavenly Father, by your own choice. But God does not want that for you. He laid out a wonderful plan for your future. All you have to do is activate the inheritance He is waiting to give you.

So Easy A Child Can Do It

Jesus said in Matthew 18:3 that, "Assuredly, I say to you, unless you are converted and become as little children, you will by no means enter the kingdom of heaven." All of this is true for understanding the mysteries of the One New Man as well. Never be too proud or caught up in your religion, tradition, and "that's-not-the-way-we-do-things" mentality that you can't see God and what He has for your tomorrow.

Walking in your inheritance is easy. However, there is a protocol for prosperity. Before you even dismiss that statement, be assured that I'm not talking about a finances-based prosperity gospel. When you prosper, everything is good, even when those who don't know Jesus might observe you and feel sorry because, by their standards, you don't have enough material possessions.

What most Christians do with the Holy Spirit and with spiritual gifts parallels what we discussed in the beginning of Chapter 8. They receive the gift of the Holy Spirit, but then just leave Him and all that He has to offer, hidden in a box.

What must you do to receive your inheritance? In Acts 26:17-18, we read the Lord's admonition to Paul:

"I will deliver you from the Jewish people, as well as from the Gentiles, to whom I now send you. To open their eyes, in order to turn them from darkness to light, and from the power of Satan to God that they may receive forgiveness of sins and an inheritance among those who are sanctified by faith in Me."

The steps to activate your inheritance are:

Be Reborn of Another From Above

To become the One New Man God has called you to be and to walk in your inheritance, you must be born into the Kingdom and live as one of its citizens. Without accepting the atoning work of Jesus Christ and making Him Lord of your entire life, nothing written in these pages, and, indeed, nothing written in the pages of any self-help, life-enriching, live-your-best-life type of book will apply to or help you.

Love The Church

To walk in this inheritance you must be among those, "who are sanctified by faith in [God]." We all know the argument, of course, that going to church doesn't make you a Christian any more than standing in a garage makes you a car, but there is no reason for a believer, born of Another from above, should ever be of the mindset that going to church is a waste of time. This is addressed in the letter to the Hebrew church when they are told to not forsake "the assembling of [y]ourselves together, as is the manner of some, but exhorting one another, and so much the more as you see the Day approaching" (Hebrews 10:25). In the simplest terms, "Go To Church!" and love being there. Because "how good and how pleasant it is for brethren to dwell together in unity!" (Psalm 133:1).

Be Sealed

There are not enough empty pages in all the world for me to be able to articulate the importance of the Baptism of the Holy Spirit in your life, walk, calling and ministry. Don't deny the Holy Spirit the opportunity to function with power in you. You must receive the Sealing or Baptism of the Holy Spirit for this is the power of God to operate in the inheritance.

Walk By Faith

Contrary to popular belief, your best is not good enough. You have to walk by faith in the supernatural work of God. You must accept who He says you are, what He says you have, what He says you can do. You can't live by what you see; you must live by His word.

There is a wonderful account in 2 Kings 6 that speaks to this very thing. The prophet Elisha and his servant had warned the king of Israel, by a Word from the Lord, of the specific plans by the Syrian king to attack certain cities.

Elisha warned the king not to venture into particular places because he might be captured or killed. The Syrian king was confounded at every turn. So much so that he accused his men of conspiring for Israel.

"Which of you has been leaking secrets to the king of Israel?" he demanded.

Shaking in their shoes, the servants protested their innocence. One stepped forward and assured his master, "None of us, my king. It is Elisha, the prophet in Israel! He tells his king the very secrets you whisper in your bedroom."

"Go and see where this Elisha is," snarled the king. "Let me know where he is, so I can *speak* with him." The servants searched high and low, scouring their network of informants. It was discovered that Elisha was in the city of Dothan. So, the king sent horses, chariots and a great army to arrive at and surround the city during the night.

When Elisha's servant awoke early the next morning and saw the city encircled by the foreboding Syrian army, he became filled with terror. He rushed to wake Elisha and begged him, "Master! We are surrounded!"

Elisha rose, walked with his servant and observed the army standing at the ready. The horses' nostrils flared as their hot breath hit the cool of the morning. The edges of swords and spears gleamed in the light of the morning sun. Elisha's servant pleaded, "They have come to kill us! What will we do?!"

Elisha reassured his servant, "Don't be afraid. The army that is with us is far greater than the one standing on the hills outside of this city." Elisha then prayed, "Lord, open his eyes and let him see."

Almost instantly, the servant gasped in shock. "What is this? The mountain is covered with fiery horses and chariots all around us!"

There was a mighty army surrounding Elisha and his servant the entire time. The prophet saw it because he was walking by faith in the promises God had given him. Elisha's servant, however, had his eyes fixed on things that could be seen in the physical. This is the downfall of men and women who refuse to walk by faith.

Closing the Book

In Rain Man, the classic movie about autism, Charlie Babbitt, played by Tom Cruise, receives notice of his father's death. He returns home to discover that millions of dollars have been left to his autistic brother, Raymond, or Rain Man.

Think about this, Charlie Babbitt missed his inheritance because he abandoned his father, disregarded his word, never understood his heart, and did not believe in what he had done. So many today are missing their inheritance because they do not like how God the Father chooses to operate.

You have been pre-destinied to enjoy a full and rich inheritance from your Maker. The choice is before you: will you simply obey your Father and receive your inheritance and be converted into the One New Man He has called you to be? Or will you make a decision to live your life according to your will, your desires, your design, and end up, like Charlie Babbit, written completely out of your Father's will?

God deeply loves you and is waiting to give you the riches of His Kingdom. The decision is yours.

THE MYSTERY OF THE ONE NEW MAN

BIBLIOGRAPHY

Adair, James R. The Old Lighthouse; the Story of the Pacific Garden Mission. Chicago: Moody Press, 1966.

Anderson, B. Ernest. "Michael Sattler: Monastic Profession, Anabaptism and the Restoration of Adult Initiation." 1990.

BrainyQuote, "Truth Quotes," BookRags Media Network (accessed June 5, 2012).

Brand, Russell. Booky Wook 2: This Time It's Personal. New York: It Books, 2010.

Clarke, Sarah Dunn. The Founding of Pacific Garden Mission: Over Thirty-Five Years Contribute to the Master's Service. Chicago: Bronson Canade Printing Company, 1914.

Comfort, Ray. The Evidence Bible: Irrefutable Evidence for the Thinking Mind. Gainesville, FL: Bridge-Logos, 2003.

David, A. Ball, M.D., Crucifixion and Death of a Man Called Jesus: From the Eyes of a Physician. Bloomington, IN: Crossbooks Publishing, 2010.

Dewey, David. A User's Guide to Bible Translations: Making the Most of Different Versions. Downers Grove, Illinois: InterVarsity Press, 2004.

Doval, Gregorio. Casualidades Coincidencias Y Serendipias De La Historia. Madrid: Ediciones Nowtilus, S.L., 2011.

Hartley, Ken. "Press On." Hixson, TN: Abba's House, 2006.

Jakes, T.D., Search Quotes (accessed June 5, 2012).

Janz, Denis. A Reformation Reader: Primary Texts with Introductions. Minneapolis, MN: Fortress Press, 1999.

Jones, Richard. Journey through the School of Groaning: A Prayer Devotional. [S.I.]: Authorhouse, 2011.

Julian, Larry S. God Is My Coach: A Business Leader's Guide to Finding Clarity in an Uncertain World. New York: Center Street, 2009.

Maillart, Ella. Forbidden Journey: From Peking to Kashmir. [United States]: Hesperides Press, 2009.

Marler, James H. "Demons Are Real?" In Reflections on the Spirit. Cleveland, TN: Alicorn Publishing, 2009.

_____. "Baptism." In Reflections on Ordinances. Cleveland, TN: Alicorn Publishing, 2011.

Martin, Mike W. Albert Schweitzer's Reverence for Life: Ethical Idealism and Self-Realization. Aldershot [u.a.]: Ashgate, 2007.

Moody, Dwight Lyman. Secret Power, or, the Secret of Success in Christian Life and Christian Work. Chicago: F.H. Revell, 1881.

Morris, Clara. Life on the Stage; My Personal Experiences and Recollections. New York: McClure, Phillips & Co., 1901.

Nee, Watchman. The Normal Christian Life. Peabody, MA: Hendrickson Publishers, Inc., 2008.

Pacific Garden, Mission. Commemorating the 50th Anniversary of Pacific Garden Mission, Inc., Chicago, IL: Everlastingly at It: Never Closed One Night in 50 Years, 1877 to 1927. Chicago, IL: The Mission, 1927.

Pink, Arthur Walkington. Studies in the Scriptures, Pensacola, FL: Mt. Zion Publications,1937.

Safire, William, and Leonard Safir. Words of Wisdom: More Good Advice. New York: Simon and Schuster, 1989.

Snyder, C. Arnold. The Life and Thought of Michael Sattler. Scottdale, PA: Herald Press, 1984.

Spader, Dann. Walking as Jesus Walked: Making Disciples the Way Jesus Did. Chicago: Moody Publishers, 2011.

Thoreau, Henry David. The Journal of Henry D. Thoreau. Vol. I. VII vols. New York, NY: Dover Publications, Inc., 1962.

Van Ryn, D.S., and M. Tabb. Mistaken Identity: Two Families, One Survivor, Unwavering Hope: Howard Books, 2008.

Voice of the, Martyrs, and John Foxe. Foxe: Voices of the Martyrs. Orlando, FL: Bridge-Logos, 2007.

Yoder, John Howard, and Michael Sattler. The Legacy of Michael Sattler. Scottdale, PA: Herald Press, 1973.

ENDNOTES

[I] Henry David Thoreau, *The Journal of Henry D. Thoreau*, VII vols., vol. I (New York, N Y: Dover Publications, Inc., 1962), 216.

[II] D.S. Van Ryn and M. Tabb, *Mistaken Identity: Two Families, One Survivor, Unwavering Hope* (Howard Books, 2008).

[III] David Dewey, *A User's Guide to Bible Translations: Making the Most of Different Versions* (Downers Grove, IL: InterVarsity Press, 2004).

[IV] All quotes obtained from BrainyQuote, "Truth Quotes," BookRags Media Network (accessed June 5, 2012).

[V] Arthur Walkington Pink, *Studies in the Scriptures, 1937* (Pensacola, FL: Mt. Zion Publications), 373.

[VI] A. Ball M.D., David, *Crucifixion and Death of a Man Called Jesus : From the Eyes of a Physician* (Bloomington, IN: Crossbooks Publishing, 2010), 65.

[VII] William Safire and Leonard Safir, *Words of Wisdom: More Good Advice* (New York: Simon and Schuster, 1989), 85.

[VIII] James R. Adair, *The Old Lighthouse; the Story of the Pacific Garden Mission* (Chicago: Moody Press, 1966)., Mission Pacific Garden, *Commemorating the 50th Anniversary of Pacific Garden Mission, Inc., Chicago, IL: Everlastingly at It: Never Closed One Night in 50 Years, 1877 to 1927* (Chicago, IL: The Mission, 1927)., and Sarah Dunn Clarke, *The Founding of Pacific Garden Mission: Over Thirty-Five Years Contribute to the Master's Service* (Chicago: Bronson Canade Printing Co., 1914).

[IX] Mike W. Martin, *Albert Schweitzer's Reverence for Life: Ethical Idealism and Self-Realization* (Aldershot [u.a.]: Ashgate, 2007), 67.

X Gregorio Doval, *Casualidades Coincidencias Y Serendipias De La Historia* (Madrid: Ediciones Nowtilus, S.L., 2011).

XI Larry S. Julian, *God Is My Coach A Business Leader's Guide to Finding Clarity in an Uncertain World* (New York: Center Street, 2009).

XII T.D. Jakes, Search Quotes (accessed June 5, 2012).

XIII Watchman Nee, *The Normal Christian Life* (Peabody, MA: Hendrickson Publishers, Inc., 2008).

XIV James H. Marler, "Baptism," in *Reflections on Ordinances* (Cleveland, TN: Alicorn Publishing, 2011).

XV Dann Spader, *Walking as Jesus Walked: Making Disciples the Way Jesus Did* (Chicago, IL: Moody Publishers, 2011).

XVI Russell Brand, *Booky Wook 2: This Time It's Personal* (New York: It Books, 2010).

XVII B. Ernest Anderson, "Michael Sattler: Monastic Profession, Anabaptism and the Restoration of Adult Initiation" (1990)., John Howard Yoder and Michael Sattler, *The Legacy of Michael Sattler* (Scottdale, PA: Herald Press, 1973)., C. Arnold Snyder, *The Life and Thought of Michael Sattler* (Scottdale, PA: Herald Press, 1984)., John Foxe, Foxe: Voices of the Martyrs (Orlando, FL: Bridge-Logos, 2007)., and Denis Janz, *A Reformation Reader : Primary Texts with Introductions* (Minneapolis, MN: Fortress Press, 1999).

XVIII James H. Marler, "Demons Are Real?," in *Reflections on the Spirit* (Cleveland, TN: Alicorn Publishing, 2009).

XIX Clara Morris, *Life on the Stage; My Personal Experiences and Recollections* (New York: McClure, Phillips & Co., 1901).

XX Dwight Lyman Moody, *Secret Power, or, the Secret of Success in Christian Life and Christian Work* (Chicago: F. H. Revell, 1881).

[XXI] Ella Maillart, *Forbidden Journey: From Peking to Kashmir* (United States: Hesperides Press, 2009).

[XXII] Ray Comfort, *The Evidence Bible: Irrefutable Evidence for the Thinking Mind* (Gainesville, FL: Bridge-Logos, 2003).

[XXIII] Ken Hartley, "Press On," (Hixson, TN: Abba's House, 2006).

[XXIV] Richard Jones, *Journey through the School of Groaning: A Prayer Devotional* (S.l.: Authorhouse, 2011).

FOR ADDITIONAL RESOURCES
OR TO SCHEDULE THE AUTHOR FOR
SPEAKING ENGAGEMENTS,
CONTACT:

DWAIN MILLER
CROSS LIFE CHURCH
1010 COMBS STREET
EL DORADO, ARKANSAS, 71730

PHONE: 870-863-7626

EMAIL: dwain@crosslifechurch.net

INTERNET: www.dwainmiller.com
www.crosslifechurch.net